1 MONTH

FREE
READING

at
www.ForgottenBooks.com

By purchasing this book you are eligible for one month membership to ForgottenBooks.com, giving you unlimited access to our entire collection of over 700,000 titles via our web site and mobile apps.

To claim your free month visit: www.forgottenbooks.com/free210940

* Offer is valid for 45 days from date of purchase. Terms and conditions apply.

Similar Books Are Available from
www.forgottenbooks.com

Beautiful Joe
An Autobiography, by Marshall Saunders

Theodore Roosevelt, an Autobiography
by Theodore Roosevelt

Napoleon
A Biographical Study, by Max Lenz

Up from Slavery
An Autobiography, by Booker T. Washington

Gotama Buddha
A Biography, Based on the Canonical Books of the Theravādin, by Kenneth J. Saunders

Plato's Biography of Socrates
by A. E. Taylor

Cicero
A Biography, by Torsten Petersson

Madam Guyon
An Autobiography, by Jeanne Marie Bouvier De La Motte Guyon

The Writings of Thomas Jefferson
by Thomas Jefferson

Thomas Skinner, M.D.
A Biographical Sketch, by John H. Clarke

Saint Thomas Aquinas of the Order of Preachers (1225-1274)
A Biographical Study of the Angelic Doctor, by Placid Conway

Recollections of the Rev. John Johnson and His Home
An Autobiography, by Susannah Johnson

Biographical Sketches in Cornwall, Vol. 1 of 3
by R. Polwhele

Autobiography of John Francis Hylan, Mayor of New York
by John Francis Hylan

The Autobiography of Benjamin Franklin
The Unmutilated and Correct Version, by Benjamin Franklin

James Mill
A Biography, by Alexander Bain

George Washington
An Historical Biography, by Horace E. Scudder

Florence Nightingale
A Biography, by Irene Cooper Willis

Marse Henry
An Autobiography, by Henry Watterson

Autobiography and Poems
by Charlotte E. Linden

797,885 Books
are available to read at

www.ForgottenBooks.com

Forgotten Books' App
Available for mobile, tablet & eReader

ISBN 978-1-331-59827-5
PIBN 10210940

This book is a reproduction of an important historical work. Forgotten Books uses state-of-the-art technology to digitally reconstruct the work, preserving the original format whilst repairing imperfections present in the aged copy. In rare cases, an imperfection in the original, such as a blemish or missing page, may be replicated in our edition. We do, however, repair the vast majority of imperfections successfully; any imperfections that remain are intentionally left to preserve the state of such historical works.

Forgotten Books is a registered trademark of FB &c Ltd.
Copyright © 2015 FB &c Ltd.
FB &c Ltd, Dalton House, 60 Windsor Avenue, London, SW19 2RR.
Company number 08720141. Registered in England and Wales.

For support please visit www.forgottenbooks.com

THE TAGORE FAMILY

A MEMOIR

BY

JAMES W. FURRELL

(SECOND EDITION)

PRINTED FOR PRIVATE CIRCULATION

CALCUTTA
PRINTED BY THACKER, SPINK & CO

1892

(The rights of translation and of reproduction are reserved.)

CALCUTTA :
PRINTED BY THACKER, SPINK AND CO.

PREFACE.

THE Memoir contained in the following pages is based mainly on materials placed at the author's disposal by the Honourable Maharaja Jotendra Mohun Tagore, and, in respect of the life of Dwarika Nath Tagore, on the biography of that gentleman published some years ago by the late Babu Kishori Chand Mittra.

Owing to the veil which the conditions of Indian society throw over the intercourse of domestic life, and to the fact that such epistolary correspondence as is preserved in native families is confined, for the most part, to matters of business devoid of interest to the outside world, it can claim to be little more than a record of the public careers of the leading members of the family whose name it bears.

In the translation of Indian names the author has adopted the scientific system wherever he felt himself at liberty to do so, the exceptions being those cases in which family usage or common custom has established a different mode of spelling.

THE TAGORE FAMILY.

It has been frequently maintained that between the genius of Western and that of Oriental culture there exists an imcompatibility so essential and profound that any attempt to combine them, if not altogether futile, must necessarily lead to results either disastrous or grotesque.

No more convincing refutation of the truth of this opinion could, perhaps, be found than has been furnished to the world by the illustrious family of Brahmans whose history forms the subject of the following pages.

If any such essential incompatibility as is alleged really existed, it is in the case of the more highly developed products of either civilisation that we should naturally expect to find it most pronounced. On such a supposition, there is no family in Bengal, or indeed in the whole of India, in which we could reasonably look for less aptitude for the assimilation of European ideas than that of the Tagores, who trace their descent from one of the most celebrated apostles of Brahmanism, the illustrious Bhatta Narayana himself, and among whom profound Sanskrit scholarship has been hereditary for nearly a thousand years.

Not only, however, do we find the Tagores conspicuous among the earliest Indian students of the English language and literature, but we shall look in vain among their countrymen for more brilliant examples of success in the practical application of such studies than their ranks have produced.

Long before knowledge of English had become a recognised passport to preferment in the public service, or the Government had afforded any special facilities for its acquisition, Darpa Narayan Tagore was a proficient not only in that language but also in French; his son, Gopee Mohun Tagore, was equally well versed in English, French, Portuguese, Persian and Urdu; while the entire career of the late Prosunna Coomar Tagore was a convincing proof that, along with the learning, he had imbibed deeply the true spirit, of Western culture.

Nor has this success in the cultivation of foreign languages and literature been attended with the reproach of having been purchased at the cost of that native scholarship which should be the first aim, as it must always be the chief and truest glory, of every patriotic Indian; for the Tagore family continues to this day to be distinguished for the same pre-eminence in Sanskrit learning that secured for its renowned ancestors the patronage of King Adisur, and raised them at once to the front rank of society in Bengal.

Hurro Coomar Tagore, the son of Gopee Mohun Tagore, was not only justly famed for his patronage of Sanskrit studies, but was himself a Sanskrit scholar of no mean eminence. Prosunna Coomar Tagore's numerous works, translated from, or based upon, Sanskrit originals, possess a wide-spread reputation. Maharajah Jotendra Mohun Tagore has enriched the literature of the day by numerous dramatic works of great merit in the vernacular, either original or translated from the classical language of the Hindus. Raja Sourendra Mohun Tagore's learned investigations into the recondite subject of Indian music have earned for him world-wide celebrity and honorary distinctions and decorations too numerous to detail.

In short, when we trace the history of the Tagore family from the days of Bhatta Narayana downwards, we may reasonably doubt whether any act of an Indian sovereign has effected more towards the development of learning and the enlightenment of posterity than Adisur's importation into Bengal of the five learned Brahmans of Kanouj.

EARLY ANCESTRY.

In writing a memoir of the Tagore family, the biographer naturally takes his start from an event so memorable in the annals of Bengal, and of their ancestry, as that just referred to.

History has left us no means of determining with absolute precision the period of the founder of the great Sena dynasty of Bengal. By combining the evidence regarding its genealogy furnished by the well-known Rājshahai inscription, which is dateless, with the statement of the author of the Samayprakāsa as to the time of the completion of the Dānāsāgara of Ballāl Sena, on the one hand, and that of the Ayin Akbarī, which places the commencement of Ballāl Sena's reign in A.D. 1066, on the other, the learned Bābu Rājendra Lāla Mittra arrives at A.D. 994 as the probable date of the accession of Vīra Sena, who was either the immediate successor of Adisura, or, as the Rājshahai inscription just referred to renders not unlikely, and as

Bābu Rājendra Lāla Mittra suggests, actually identical with that renowned monarch.

Without aiming at precision, where precision is, in the existing state of our knowledge, unattainable, we may reasonably accept the latter part of the tenth century of the Christian era as an adequate approximation to the period of Adisur.

Regarding the manner of Adisur's accession to the throne of Bengal, we know as little as about the exact date of that celebrated event. This much, however, is established by a concurrence of testimony—that he conquered the country from a Buddhist sovereign, and that Buddhism had then been the religion of the Court at Gaur long enough to bring about a very general decay of Brahminical institutions and learning in Bengal.

Tradition runs that, some time after his accession, Adisur, owing to the occurrence in his dominions of severe famine and other portents, which he regarded as evidence of the divine displeasure, determined to perform certain expiatory sacrifices. So complete, however, had been the neglect of Brahminical learning and practice among his subjects, that no Brahmans competent to celebrate the necessary rites were to be found in his territories; and Adisur, having consulted Gunārām Bhatta, a minister of his Court, resolved to apply to Vīra Sinha, the reigning monarch of Kanouj, to send him qualified Brahmans for the purpose.

Vīra Sinha accordingly selected five Brahmans, Bhatta Narayana, Daksha, Vedagarbha, Chhandara, and Sri Harsha for the task, and despatched them to Adisur.

On their arrival at his capital, the story proceeds, Adisur, having ascertained, from the reports made him by his officers, that they had come riding on bulls, with their sacred threads made of leather; that they allowed their beards and whiskers to grow; chewed betel, and in other respects departed from the usual practice of orthodox Brahmans, received them with coldness, if not disrespect; and the result was that they made up their minds to return to Kanouj. Unwilling, however, to leave without first making some attempt to convince the king of his error and vindicate their own reputation, they placed certain sacrificial offerings on a dry tree in the neighbourhood of the king's palace; and no sooner had they done so than the withered trunk sent forth both branches and leaves.

Assured by this miracle of the sanctity of his guests, Adisur now hastened to welcome them and bring them into his palace.

Thereupon Bhatta Narayana, who appears to have been recognised as the chief of the five Brahmans, presented the King with a drama which he had composed, under the title of 'Beni Samhara,' on the subject of the great war between the Kurus and the Pāndabas.

After the sacrifice had been performed, the five Brahmans, according to some, returned to Kanouj, laden with presents; but, finding that they had lost caste with their fellow-tribesmen by their late journey, they made up their minds to settle permanently in Bengal. They accordingly repaired again to the Court of Adisur, who, as a reward for their services and a solatium for their exile, bestowed on them grants of five villages in the Rārha country, where they proceeded to take up their abode.

Such is the story of the migration of the Kanouj Brahmans to Gaur. Whatever doubt may attach to its details, its main features are as little open to question as is the influence which the event exercised on the subsequent development of society in Bengal.

Of the subsequent career of Daksha, Vedagarbha, and Chhandara tradition has little to say, though among the ten noble families so recognised by Ballāla Sena, who was probably the fifth in descent from Adisur, and who reigned towards the close of the eleventh century, six were descendants of one or other of these three Brahmans.

Bhatta Narayana is reputed to have left sixteen sons, among whom was Nri Sinha, or Nānu, a Suddha Srotriya, the ancestor of the

Thākurs, or, as the name has been anglicised, the Tagores.

Of his posterity, the first who occupies a conspicuous place in tradition is Dhāranidhāra, who is said to have been the eighth in descent, and is known as the author of a 'Commentary on the Institutes of Menu.' His brother, Banamāli, was also a distinguished author.

Dhāranidhāra had a grandson, Dhananjay, who occupied the office of judge under Ballāla Sena, and was also the author of a Vedic vocabulary, entitled the *Nighanta*.

The social influence which, owing to the commanding acquirements and merits of the Kanouj Brahmans, would probably have been great under any circumstances, was accentuated by the system of Kulinism established by Ballāla Sena.

'The main object of this system,' says Bābu Rājendra Lāla Mittra, 'was to give pre-eminence to the descendants of the five Brahmans and Kāyasthas who had been brought to Bengal by Adisura. The particular qualities which were to characterise his nobles were "good manners, learning, humility, reputation, pilgrimage, faith, fixed profession, austerity, and charity," but, as there was no standard measure for these qualities, and it was difficult to secure them without attaching penalties to personal delinquencies which could never be enforced, he had recourse to other and more definite means for their perpetuation. He availed himself of the popular notion that children invariably inherit the moral qualities of their parents, and hoped that by maintaining the blood of his newly created nobles pure and undefiled, he would attain his end. He forbade all intermarriages between the original Brahmans and Kāyasthas of the country and the new-comers, and ordained various and complicated rules for the gradual degradation of those families which should permit any stain to fall on the gentility of their blood.'

We next come to his son, Halayudha, who was Prime Minister to Lakshman Sena, the successor of Ballāla Sena, and who is known as the author of many valuable works, including the 'Brahmana,' 'Sarvasa,' the 'Nayaya,' 'Pandita,' 'Shiva,' 'Matsya,' and 'Sakta Tantra,' the 'Avidhāna Ratnamālā,' and the 'Kabi Rahasya.'

The above genealogy, it will be seen, makes Halayudha the twelfth in descent from Bhatta Narayana, while Lakshman Sena, in whose reign he flourished, is, according to Bābu Rājendra Lāla Mittra's table of the Sena kings, only the fifth in descent from Adisur. A discrepancy is thus disclosed which it is impossible to reconcile, and which seems to suggest that either the number of generations between Adisur and Lakshman Sena must be considerably increased, or Halayudha must be placed much nearer to Bhatta Narayana. The fact that nothing is known regarding the first seven descendants of Nri Sinha may, perhaps, be considered to favour the latter alternative. The number of generations between Bhatta Narayana and the present representatives of the Tagores would thus be reduced to twenty-six or twenty-seven.

Through his son, Bivu, Halayudha had two grandsons, Mahendra and Ganendra, who were respectively known as the Bara and Chhotā Kumār, a title usually restricted to the sons of Rajas.

Raja Rām, the fourth in descent from Mahendra, and his grandson, Jagannātha, were both authors of repute, and the latter was honoured with the title of Paṇḍit-Raja, or Prince of Pandits.

His son, Purushottam, again, wrote a large number of learned works, including the 'Prayāga Ratnamālā,' the 'Mukti Chintā-mani,' the 'Bhāsā Briti' the Taikānda Shesha,' the 'Ekasāra Kosha,' the 'Hār-latā,' the 'Haraboli,' and the 'Gotrapravara Darpana.'

In spite of his great learning, Purushottam was destined to cast a blot on the escutcheon of his descendants by contracting a marriage with the daughter of a man who, otherwise of unstained reputation, had, according to the decision of the pandits, incurred forfeiture of caste by the accidental smelling of forbidden food. While, however, the flaw thus introduced into the pedigree of the family has in no degree affected the respect in which they are held by their countrymen, it has invested them with the right of making their own caste laws, and thus conferred on them an immunity from vexatious restrictions which they would not otherwise have enjoyed, and of which, as we shall see later on, they have not been slow to avail themselves.

Learning still continued to be hereditary in the family, and Bolorām, the son of Purushottam, added the 'Prohodha Prakāsa' to the long list of works they had already given to the world.

Panchānana, the fifth in descent from Bolorām, appears to have been the first member of the family who received the title of Thākur, which, in its corrupted form of Tagore, they still continue to bear.

Having left Jessore, which, since the

time of Purushottam, had been the adopted home of the family, he came to the village of Govindpur, on the banks of the Hughli, purchased a piece of land there, and built on it a dwelling-house and a temple, which, true to his ancestral cult, he dedicated to the god Siva.

Here he came into intimate contact with the future conquerors of Hindustan, and, being a man of parts, soon succeeded in establishing himself in their favour and confidence. Thus he had no difficulty in procuring for his son, Joyrām, the appointment of Amin of the Twenty-four Parganehs, a post which, imposing on him as it did the duty of conducting the settlement, as well as collecting the revenue, of that important district, was one of considerable responsibility.

The capture of Calcutta by the infamous Siraj-ud-Daulah interrupted for a time his progress towards fortune. The loss which he suffered on the occasion was, however, destined to be more than compensated. For when, after the retaking of the place, it became necessary to construct a new fort, the site selected for the purpose was that on which Panchānan had built the family house and temple. The buildings were accordingly purchased by the Government, and other land was given to Joyrām in exchange for that taken up by them at Govindpur. Joyram thereupon removed to Calcutta; and, having purchased a fresh site on the river bank at Pathariaghatta, there erected a new dwelling-house and bathing ghāt, which are the property of his descendants to this day.

He also appears to have been associated in some way with the construction of the new fort, and may possibly have derived some pecuniary advantage from the connexion. Certain it is that, during the latter part of his life, he found the means of retrieving the losses which he had suffered at the time of the taking of Calcutta.

Joyrām died in the year 1762, and left four sons—Ananda Rām, Darpa Narāyan, Nilmoni, and Gobinda Rām.

The first and last of these died without

issue; but Darpa Narayan and Nilmoni both left sons.

Darpa Narāyan, whose career will be noticed more in detail hereafter, remained at home, and, entering into commercial and land transactions, acquired a large fortune. Nilmoni chose the service of the British Government, and eventually rose to the Serishtadarship of the District Court.

On his retirement from official life he became involved in a dispute with his more fortunate brother regarding the amount of certain sums of money which he remitted him from time to time for safe keeping; and in the end, as the result of a compromise, received from him on this account, and in lieu of his share in the paternal property, the sum of a lakh of rupees. Separating thereupon from his brother, he built a family house for himself at Jorasanko, on a site said to have been granted him by Boystom Dās Seth, as a testimony to his piety.

Nilmoni had three sons, Rām Lochan, Rām Moni, and Rām Ballabh.

Rām Moni had three sons, of whom the celebrated Dwārikā Nāth Tagore was the second, and Roma Nāth Tagore the third.

Rām Lochan, having no child of his own, adopted Dwārikā Nāth Tagore, an excellent account of whose career was published by the late Babu Kishori Chand Mittra.

Dwarika Nath Tagore.

Like his illustrious cousin, Prosunna Coomar Tagore, Dwārikā Nāth Tagore was indebted for the elements of an English education to Mr. Sherbourne, who in those days kept a school in the Chitpore Road, Calcutta. The course of study pursued at this institution seems, however, to have been of a very humble character, and Dwārikā Nāth probably owed much more to the instruction of the Rev. William Adams, who subsequently acted as his tutor, and to the friendly intercourse which, even as a young man, he maintained with Europeans of education and position.

A circumstance which had a still greater share in the formation of his character, was his early association with the great Hindu reformer, Rām Mohun Roy.

The active philanthropy which characterised his career was, no doubt, the expression of his own inborn beneficence of temperament; but in the catholicity with which that philanthropy was exercised, as well as in the entire freedom from bigotry or narrowness which has own personal conduct exhibited, the influence of the new teacher may be clearly traced.

Dwārikā Nāth's first experience of the practical business of life was in the management of the modest estates inherited by him from his father. Brought thus into frequent contact with the courts of the country, he became a diligent student of the law; and, having attained to extraordinary proficiency in this branch of learning, he after a time established himself as a law agent. In this capacity he rapidly achieved a reputation which brought him a numerous and wealthy *clientèle* among the landed proprietary both of Bengal and of the North-Western Provinces.

So great, however, was his capacity for work, and so many-sided was his genius, that he was able to conduct at the same time, and with no less conspicuous success, an extensive commercial agency.

In the midst of all this prosperity the post of Serishtadar to the Salt Agent and Collector of the Twenty-four Parganehs became vacant, and, tempted by the prestige which service under the Government conferred, Dwārikā Nāth was induced to accept it. How completely he gained the confidence of his superiors is shown by his promotion, six years later, to the Diwanship of the Board of Customs, Salt, and Revenue, which office he filled for several years with distinguished credit.

Such a career, however, was too contracted and too fettered for a man of Dwārikā Nāth's large designs and independent character. In 1834, on the ground of the pressure of private business, he, to the great regret of the Board, resigned an appointment which he had filled with exceptional ability; and soon after, in partnership with

Mr. William Carr and Mr. William Prinsep, established the firm of Carr, Tagore, and Co.

He was thus the first native gentleman to enter into mercantile business in Calcutta on the European model; and the Governor-General of the day, Lord William Bentinck, considered the event of sufficient importance to make it the subject of a congratulatory letter to the author of so praiseworthy an example.

With the original partners in the new firm were subsequently associated, at one time or another, Major H. B. Henderson, Mr. W. C. M. Plowden, Dr. Macpherson, Captain Taylor, Babu Debendra Nāth Tagore, and Babu Girendra Nāth Tagore; while Babu Prosunna Coomar Tagore was for some time one of its assistants.

Previously to the establishment of the firm of Carr, Tagore, and Co., Dwārikā Nāth had been associated with Messrs. J. G. Gordon, J. Calder, John Palmer, and Colonel James Young in founding the famous and ill-fated Union Bank, of which Babu

Ramanath Tagore was treasurer, and which during his lifetime enjoyed a career of remarkable and almost unchequered prosperity, to collapse hopelessly not long after his death. Of the only two other banks, besides the Bank of Bengal, then existing in Calcutta, the Calcutta Bank was absorbed by the Union, and the Commercial Bank was closed, on the failure of Messrs. Macintosh and Co. in 1829, Dwārikā Nāth, as the only solvent partner, having to meet all the claims against it.

Dwārikā Nāth was the mainstay of the Union Bank, and on more than one occasion interposed with his ample purse to save it from losses which would have injured its credit, if not landed it in ruin.

The firm of Carr, Tagore, and Co. at once took a place in the front rank of Calcutta houses, and embarked largely, after the manner of those days, in indigo, silk, and other commercial enterprises in the interior. As to Dwārikā Nāth, his rapidly-increasing fortune enabled him to purchase numerous zemindaries in Rajshahai, Pabna, Rangpur, Jessore, Cuttack, and other districts.

A memoir which should be merely a record of the assiduous energy, the bold enterprise, and the unvaried skill which enabled Dwārikā Nāth to achieve a success in the practical affairs of life almost without precedent among his countrymen, would be but an imperfect account of the career of a man who contributed more largely than any of his contemporaries to the wonderful social progress which marked the history of Bengal during the first half of the present century; a man of whom the *Times*, commenting on his death, justly said that his name would 'be proudly associated with all the noble institutions flourishing in Calcutta.'

Reference has been made in general terms to his catholic philanthropy. It remains to give some account of the manner in which this philanthropy was exercised, and the results which have attended it.

'When Dwārikā Nāth saw light,' says the late Kishori Chand Mittra, in his eloquent biography, 'ignorance and superstition reigned rampant. The Hindoo widows were immolated at the funeral pile of their husbands; the natives were persecuted and proscribed as a subject race; the dark fatality of a dark skin crushed and kept them down; the crime of colour was considered the most atrocious in the social and political code governing the country; the community was divided into sahib logues and natives. These two classes, composing the dominant few and the subject many. not understanding each other, were estranged and alienated. Now what did Dwārikā Nāth leave behind? A Hindoo College and a Medical College; the revolting rite of suttee abolished and branded by law as murder; a Landholders' Society, representing a most important interest in the country; steam communication; a free Press; an uncovenanted judicial service; a subordinate executive service; and a better understanding between the Natives and the Europeans—being the first step to a fusion of the two races.'

In the inception, or in the completion, of each and all of the reforms on which the above contrast depends, Dwārikā Nāth Tagore took a leading or an important part.

Dwārikā Nāth was an enthusiastic advocate of that downward filtration theory of native education which from the time of Lord Bentinck to a very late period entirely dominated, and still largely influences, the Government scheme of public instruction, as well as of the view that the English language is the only suitable vehicle of higher education in Bengal. As a member of the committee of management of the Hindoo College, he took an active part in the reorganisation of that institution, and its erection into 'a seminary of the highest possible description for the cultivation of the English language.'

No less intimate was his connexion with the success of the Medical College, which was founded on June 1, 1835. In the first year of its existence he placed at the disposal of its governing body the sum of two thousand rupees a year for three years, for distribution in the form of prizes to native students of merit. But, what was of still greater importance in its influence on the medical education of his countrymen, and reflected yet higher honour on him, was the self-sacrificing devotion with which, when the strong prejudice of the Hindoo students against taking part in the operations of the dissecting-room threatened to mar the usefulness of the College, he threw himself into the gap, and by his own frequent presence taught his co-religionists to feel that the interests of science in the cause of humanity were paramount to the promptings of personal inclination, or the voice of national tradition.

In his efforts for the abolition of the cruel rite of suttee, Rām Mohun Roy found in his friend, Dwārikā Nāth, a zealous and powerful coadjutor. But for his support, the Government might well have hesitated to show the courage of its convictions, and lay the axe to the root of a custom which the great mass of the people regarded as vitally associated with the foundations of morality and religion. Less disinterested, perhaps, but none the less creditable to his public spirit, was the leading part taken by Dwārikā Nāth in the foundation of the Landholders' Society, which was at once recognised by the Government of Bengal as a channel of communication with the zemindars, and which for a long time exercised an important influence on its land legislation.

In the agitation which ultimately led to the establishment of regular steam communication between India and England, Dwārikā Nāth took a prominent share; and throughout the discussion regarding the Press laws he was in the front rank of the champions of freedom.

Against the Press Act of 1824 he fought, at considerable cost to himself, an ineffectual fight; and at the great public meeting held on January 5, 1835, to petition Lord William Bentinck for its abolition, we find him one of the principal speakers.

He it was who seconded the resolution

moved by Mr. T. Dickens, that the petition be adopted.

'In rising to second the resolution that this petition be adopted,' he said, 'I am only doing that which I did ten years ago. When this Regulation was first promulgated, I, with three of my own relations, and my lamented friend the late Rām Mohun Roy, were the only persons who petitioned the Supreme Court against it; but most sincerely do I congratulate the community at large that I now see the whole room of the Town Hall filled both with Europeans and Natives for the purpose of protesting against the Regulation. At that time I did not ask any European to sign a petition, his signature to which might have subjected him to transportation. The same objection, however, did not exist in the case of the Natives, for the Government, even at that day, could hardly have transported them. But none of the Natives could I prevail upon to join me, and I believe it was thought that I should be hanged the next day for my boldness.

'I think the present is the very time we ought to petition against the Regulation, because for the last eight years we have, under the rule of Lord William Bentinck, enjoyed a really free Press in spite of its provisions. If we could only secure Lord William Bentinck as a Governor-General, there would be no need of a petition, for with him this law is a dead letter, as well as many of the Court of Directors' laws; but we do not know whom we may get next, and, for anything we can tell to the contrary, Mr. Sutherland and Mr. Stocqueler may be turned out by the next Governor-General. This, then, is the time when we ought to petition; and I have every hope, from the known character of Lord William Bentinck, and from the interest he has always taken in the welfare of the Natives, and in that of the community at large, that he will repeal the Regulation; and, when once it is repealed, I think it will be difficult for any future Governor-General to get it enacted again.'

Though the Regulation was not repealed

before Lord William Bentinck laid down the reins of office, the fear that his successor might prove less liberal was not realised; and, just five months later, another public meeting, in which Babu Dwārikā Nāth Tagore again took a prominent part, was held at the Town Hall, to thank the new Governor-General, Sir Charles Metcalfe, for the removal of all legal restrictions on the freedom of the Press.

At the dinner given in 1838 to commemorate this measure, the health of Dwārikā Nāth was proposed by Mr. Parker, as one whose name was inseparably connected with the cause whose triumph they had met that night to celebrate.

It is to the suggestion of Dwārikā Nāth Tagore, put forward in his evidence before the Committee on the Reform of the Mufasal Police, that Bengal owes the creation of the office of deputy-magistrate, in which so many of his fellow-countrymen have since been able to perform valuable service in the cause of law and order. The suggestion was heartily approved of by the Government and soon after carried into effect, several Native gentlemen of good family and distinguished pupils of the Hindoo College being appointed to the new office.

In the agitation against what was called the 'Black Act,' Babu Dwārikā Nāth Tagore took a prominent part, and he was one of the principal speakers at the public meeting held in the Town Hall on June 18, 1836, for the purpose of memorialising the Court of Directors and Board of Control to repeal Act XI of that year, by which European British subjects were deprived of their right of appeal to the supreme courts against the decisions of the Mufasal tribunals.

By his vehement denunciation of the state of the latter on this occasion, he did quite as great a service to his own countrymen as to the class whose interests were specially affected by the obnoxious Act in question.

It may be regarded as a proof of the estimation in which Dwārikā Nāth was held by the Government, that he was the first native of India who was appointed a Justice of the Peace, an honour which possessed a much greater significance in those days than it does now. As a matter of fact, he was constantly consulted by Lord Auckland as an exponent of Native opinion, and was a frequent guest of the Governor-General at his country-house at Barrackpore.

His own hospitality, which was largely extended to Europeans of position, was as highly appreciated as it was profuse, and the entertainments which he was in the habit of giving, on a grand scale, at his villa at Belgatchia, were without rival in their day.

At the close of the year 1841, Dwārikā Nāth made up his mind to visit England, for which country he embarked on January 9 following, amid general valedictions from all classes of the community.

His approaching departure from Calcutta was the occasion of a public meeting at the Town Hall, presided over by the Sheriff, at which a most complimentary address to the hero of the hour was moved by Mr. (afterwards Sir) Thomas Turton, and seconded by Mr. Mansel, of the Civil Service, the Deputy Accountant-General.

This meeting, which was the first of its kind ever held in Calcutta, was attended by most of the principal residents of the city, European and Native.

In replying to the address, Dwārikā Nath said : 'Gentlemen, this is a proud moment for me and for my country. It is the first time that a native of India has ever received such a testimony of regard from the inhabitants of our Eastern metropolis. The main object of my life has been to improve my native land. I viewed, as the best means of effecting this great object, the charitable institutions and social habits of Great Britain. The initiative efforts had already been made by others, and particularly by my lamented friend, the late Rām Mohun Roy. Knowing how imperfect my endeavours have been, I feel conscious that your approbation is rather applicable to the attempt than to any success which is fairly ascribable to me. The good work, however, has commenced, to whomsoever be the praise, and my hopes are high for the result. Proud am I, indeed, that my motives and conduct should have been so appreciated and rewarded by my fellow-citizens, both of England and of India.

'The expression of your sentiments is doubly grateful to me, for, while it is a matter of the highest congratulation to me, it is not less so to my countrymen. It proves to them and to the world at large how closely the landholders of England and India are united in feelings and in interests, when the humble efforts of a Hindoo are thus rewarded by the united approbation of the British community, as well as by his own beloved brethren of his native land. Most heartily do I thank you, gentlemen, for the honour you have conferred, and the flattering terms in which it has been expressed. The little which I have been enabled to do, if not aided by your kind and friendly feeling, would not have entitled me to the kind and flattering distinction of my likeness being placed in the hall of your city. But I will cheerfully accept of the proud distinction, in the hope that it may stimulate others of my countrymen to follow in a course which you have so generously rewarded.'

On January 11, the 'India' left the Sandheads with Dwārikā Nāth and his party, consisting of Dr. MacGowan, his medical attendant; Chunder Mohun Chatterjea, his nephew; Purmananda Moittra, his personal attendant; and four servants. Sir Edward Ryan and Archbishop Carew were among his fellow passengers.

During the voyage he kept a diary, which, while marked by a certain *naïveté*, not unnatural under the circumstances, displays no little intelligence and power of observation.

On February 11 the vessel reached Suez, and on the following day Dwārikā Nāth and his party started for Cairo, which they reached on the 14th. Leaving Cairo on the 24th, in a small steamer, they reached Alexandria the following day. On April 1 they arrived at Malta, whence they embarked on the 11th in the 'Polyphemus,' for Italy.

After a rough passage, Dwārikā Nāth arrived at Naples on the 14th, and left again on the 21st, for Rome, which he reached on the 23rd, travelling by the road.

As might have been expected, the latter city impressed him greatly.

'Description,' he says, in a letter to a friend in Calcutta, 'can convey but very faint ideas of its beauty. Everything is on a grand scale, and St. John's Church, with which I was so pleased at Malta, and also those at Naples, sink into insignificance when compared with St. Peter's, which in size alone would contain about twenty of them, and is far superior in elegance and decoration. One might visit it daily, and always find something new and pleasing to admire. So are the museum, the library, the ruins, statues, paintings, fountains. No doubt Rome stands peerless as far as grandeur and beauty are concerned.'

At Rome Dwārikā Nāth had the honour of being received by the Pope, and, at a party at Colonel Caldwell's, he met Prince Frederick of Prussia and Mrs. Somerville, the mathematician and astronomer.

From Rome he proceeded to Venice, visiting Florence, among other places, by the way. Thence he travelled, *viâ* Trent, into Germany, passing through Stuttgard, Heidelberg, Frankfort, and Mayence to Cologne. From Cologne he travelled by railway to Aix-la-Chapelle, from which place he went to Brussels and Ostend, and, posting thence to Calais, embarked there for Dover on June 9.

Arriving in London on the following day, he took up his residence in the first instance at St. George's Hotel, Albemarle Street, but subsequently removed to the house of Mr. William Prinsep's mother, in Great Cumberland Street.

His reputation, and the letters of introduction he carried with him to many of the most distinguished persons in the country, secured him a magnificent reception wherever he went. The Court of Directors, as became them, entertained him at a public dinner at the London Tavern; and, having been presented to the Queen at the Drawing-room held on June 16, he was, a week later, commanded to dine at Buckingham Palace.

'Besides Her Majesty and Prince Albert,' says Babu Kishori Chand Mittra, in his biography, 'there were present at the Royal party Prince and Princess of Saxe-Coburg-Gotha, Earl of Liverpool, Lord Fitzgerald, Cooper, Bart.' (Sir Astley Cooper ?) 'and Baron de Brandestine. Her Majesty and the Prince Consort entered into an interesting conversation with Dwārikā Nāth, of which the themes were chiefly Indian. He then played a game at whist with the Duchess of Kent. Her Majesty presented him with three new pieces of golden coin which had been minted that day.'

Subsequently he was invited by the Queen to pay a visit to the Royal nursery, where the Princess Royal and the Prince of Wales were brought out to see him.

Among members of the nobility who entertained him at dinner were the Marquis of Lansdowne and Lord Lyndhurst; and he attended a grand review of the troops at the special invitation of Her Majesty. He was also a guest at the Lord Mayor's annual dinner, the Duke of Cambridge, the Duke of Buccleuch, and several of the ministers being present on the occasion. The Lord Mayor proposed his health, remarking, in the course of his speech: 'The high character and great attainments of my friend on my right render him an ornament to society. The great kindness he has shown to our countrymen in India entitles him to the gratitude of every British subject.'

Dwārikā Nāth acknowledged the toast in an eloquent speech, which occupied half an hour in delivery.

After seeing the chief sights of London, Dwārikā Nāth left for the manufacturing districts, visiting Sheffield, York, Newcastle,

Edinburgh, Glasgow, Liverpool, Birmingham, Worcester, and Bristol during his tour. At Edinburgh he was admitted as a Burgess and Guild Brother of the City, and presented with addresses by the Unitarian Association and the Emigration and Aborigines Protection Society.

At Newcastle he was much interested in the mines, of which he gives a minute account in his diary.

On his return to London, he received a command from the Queen to lunch with her at Windsor Palace, on which occasion Her Majesty and the Prince Consort consented, at his request, to sit for the full-length portraits which now adorn the Town Hall of Calcutta. At the same time the Queen ordered miniature portraits of herself and Prince Albert to be prepared for presentation to Dwārikā Nāth himself.

On October 16 Dwārikā Nāth left England for France, arriving at Paris on the 18th.

There he made the acquaintance of many

distinguished persons, and was honoured with an interview with Louis Philippe and the Queen, and with the King and Queen of Belgium.

While in Paris he received a gold medal from the Directors of the East India Company, in recognition of his services to his country.

This medal was accompanied by the following letter :—

' SIR,—On the occasion of your return to your native country, the Court of Directors of the East India Company are desirous of presenting you with a testimonial of their esteem, and of the approbation with which they regard the public benefits conferred by you on British India, by the liberal encouragement you have afforded to the diffusion of education, and to the introduction of the arts and sciences; and by the generous support you have given to the charitable institutions of Calcutta, whether established for the relief of the Hindoo or British community. The Court trusts that the noble course which you have pursued will have the effect of contributing to the accomplishment of that object which it has ever been their anxious desire to promote, viz. the identification of the feelings and interests of the Natives to their Government, and thus strengthening the bond which unites India with Great Britain.

'Impressed with these sentiments, the Court requests your acceptance of a gold medal, for the preparation of which they have given the necessary instructions.

'In making this communication on their behalf, permit us to assure you of the satisfaction which we derive from being the medium of conveying the Court's feelings and wishes, in which we most fully participate; and to express our sincere hope that your visit to this country has been productive to you of much gratification, and that your future career may be marked by happiness and prosperity.'

The close of the year 1842 saw Dwārikā Nāth back in Calcutta, accompanied by Mr.

George Thompson, whom he had invited to visit India.

On his return Hindoo orthodoxy entered its protest against what it considered his violation of the rules of caste, in crossing the sea and eating with outcasts, by requiring him to perform the expiatory ceremony of Prāyaschittra, under pain of excommunication. But he refused to comply with its demands, and after a considerable amount of agitation the movement was abandoned.

Schemes for promoting the education of Hindoo women, and for raising the status of the Medical College, in which he had always taken so profound an interest, now engaged his attention.

An attempt to establish a school for Hindoo girls under European female teachers fell through; but an offer made by Dwārikā Nāth to pay the passages of two Bengali students of the Medical College to England, and the expense of educating them there, was readily accepted, and supplemented by a similar offer on the part of the Government. Four youths, including Bholā Nāth Bose and Surjee Coomar (afterwards Dr. Goodeve), Chackrabatti (Chuckerbutty), accordingly proceeded to England to complete their studies there under the care of Dr. Goodeve, and ultimately obtained the diploma of the Royal College of Surgeons.

After starting the Bengal Coal Company, in conjunction with Mr. Deans Campbell, Dwārikā Nāth again embarked for England on March 8, 1845.

The vessel which conveyed him from Calcutta was the Peninsular and Oriental Company's steamer 'Bentinck,' and he was accompanied by his youngest son, Nogendronath, his nephew, Nobin Chunder Mookerjee, his private physician, Dr. Raleigh, and his secretary, Mr. Safe.

At Cairo he had several interviews with Mehemet Ali Pacha, the Egyptian Viceroy, by whom he was warmly and honourably received.

After being detained a fortnight in quarantine at Malta, he proceeded in H.M.S. 'Aigle,' commanded by Lord Clarence Paget, and towed by a steamer placed at his disposal by the Governor, to Naples; whence, after making the ascent of Vesuvius, he set out for Paris, *viâ* Leghorn, Civita Vecchia, Pisa, Genoa, Marseilles, and Bordeaux. At Paris, where he was a frequent guest of Louis Philippe, he remained a fortnight, and arrived in London on June 24.

His first concern was to make arrangements for the education of his son and nephew. The former he accordingly placed with Dr. Drummond, and for the latter he obtained a situation as assistant in the firm of Robert Michael and Co.

Soon after his arrival, he was received at a Drawing-room at Buckingham Palace· and subsequently, on the occasion of a visit made by special invitation to the Palace, he was presented with miniature portraits of Her Majesty and the Prince Consort, together with an autograph.

In the autumn he crossed over to Ireland, in which country he made an extended tour, visiting, among other places, besides the capital, Belfast, Cork, and the Lakes of

Killarney. He dined with the Viceroy at Dublin, inspected Lord Rosse's monster telescope, and interviewed Daniel O'Connell and the apostle of temperance, Father Matthew.

Towards the end of June 1846, after his return to London, Dwārikā Nāth began to betray symptoms of failing health; and on the 30th of that month, when dining at the house of the Duchess of Inverness, he had a severe attack of ague. A change of air to Worthing was unattended by any improvement, and he returned to London, to die there on August 1, at the comparatively early age of fifty-one.

The question of the mode in which his obsequies should be performed was the subject of some hesitation and anxiety; but it was finally decided, with the acquiescence of his son, that he should be buried at Kensal Green. There, accordingly, in the unconsecrated portion of the cemetery, the remains of the Great Indian philanthropist were interred, without any religious ceremony, in the presence of his son, Nogendronath, his nephew,

Sir Edward Ryan, Major Henderson, General Ventura, Drs. Goodeve and Raleigh, Mr. W. A. Prinsep, Mr. R. Roberts, Mr. Plowden Mohun Lal, and the Hindoo Medical students who were pursuing their studies in London at his expense.

'The funeral,' says Babu Kishori Chand Mittra, 'was also attended by four royal carriages, and the equipages of many of the nobility.'

Among the numerous letters of condolence which were written to his son was the following from the Duchess of Somerset :—

'MY DEAR NOGENDRO,—I cannot tell you how I feel for you and all your family under this *most heavy* bereavement. May God support and comfort you and yours. I trust your health may not suffer from so much anxiety and constant fatigue. The Duke and I feel this sad blow, and I feel indeed as if I had lost a very near and dear friend, and I am very, very unhappy. But I will not intrude upon you at this time; only believe *how* anxiously we feel for you, and do tell me if in anything I can be of the smallest comfort or use to you; you have only to command my poor services. Accept of my *heartfelt* sympathy and our most kind remembrances, and believe me always, my dear Nogendro,

'Your very sincere and anxious friend,

(Sd.) ' M. Somerset.'

The Press noticed the sad occurrence in terms most appreciative of the merits of the deceased. The *Times* said · 'The claim that this illustrious personage has on the present generation is for his unbounded philanthropy. No reference to creed stayed his purse in the cause of charity or the advancement of education, in the promotion of colleges, whether for Native or Christian; and his name will be proudly associated with all the noble institutions flourishing in Calcutta. He had an extraordinary power of self-control, far beyond those participating in his own religion, to illustrate which it will suffice to instance his devoted encouragement to surgery. When the college for Hindoo youths for the study of anatomy was opened, Dwārikā Nāth was personally present, and witnessed the dissection of a subject—an abhorrence of the gravest nature in the eyes of the bigot portion of India—and heroically suppressed the sickness of heart and body he instinctively felt, for no other motive than that he conceived he was furthering the advancement of science, and doing a duty to mankind. He went through the ordeal with an unflinching nerve, which had its weight with those of his own particular religion who were there on the occasion.'

The *Morning Herald* observed: 'Dwarkanath Tagore had made a great step in advance; he had done more good than if he had addressed to his countrymen a score of volumes full of profound philosophical reflections.

> 'Tis in the advance of individual minds,
> That the slow crowd should ground their expectation
> Eventually to follow ; as the sea
> Waits aye in its bed, till some one wave
> Of all the multitudinous mass extends
> The empire of the whole, some feet perhaps,
> Its fellows so long time ; thenceforth the rest,
> E'en to the meanest, hurry in at once,
> And so much is clear gained.

Lines such as these might well be inscribed upon Dwarkanath Tagore's tomb. He has made an advance, the one wave before its fellows; and the rest must in due course follow.'

In Calcutta the news of his death was received with wide-spread regret by all classes of the community; and on December 2 a public meeting, presided over by Sir Peter Grant, was held at the Town Hall, to perpetuate his memory and give expression to the general sorrow.

A resolution was proposed by Archdeacon Dealtry and carried unanimously: 'That this meeting publicly record the high estimation which they entertain of the benevolent qualities of their lamented fellow-citizen, Dwārikā Nāth Tagore, and their deep regret at his untimely death. Accumulating vast wealth by talent and assiduity, he liberally employed it in charitable and national objects; whilst in private life his advice and aid was at every applicant's command, and his house was a home not only to his own countrymen, but to Europeans of every nation.'

This was followed by a resolution proposed by the Advocate-General, Mr. J. W. Colvile, seconded by Raja Satto Charan Ghosal, and also carried unanimously : ' That a subscription be entered into for the purpose of raising funds, to be vested in the name of trustees of the Dwārikā Nāth Tagore Endowment, to procure for the native youths of India, at the University College, London, the benefit of European education, either general or professional.'

A third resolution constituted the President of the Council of Education for the time being, the Advocate-General for the time being, the Government Agent for the time being, and the Secretary to the Government of Bengal for the time being, the trustees of the Dwārikā Nāth Tagore Endowment · while, by a fourth, the official trustees, Rustumjee Cowasjee, Russomoy Dutt, Rām Gopal Ghose, Dr. John Grant, Major Henderson, Rām Chunder Mitter, and Dr W. B. O'Shaughnessy were appointed members of the Committee.

Babu Dwārikā Nāth Tagore was a patriot of the truest type. To a deep solicitude for the welfare and advancement of his countrymen he united a knowledge of their necessities, as practical as it was intimate. Endowed by nature with Herculean energy and possessed of princely means, he spared neither the one nor the other to promote the cause he had at heart. A lively sympathy with the spirit of modern progress made the participation of his fellow-countrymen, as far as their circumstances might permit, in the blessings of Western civilisation, the great object of his efforts. Next to his benevolence, perhaps, the most conspicuous feature in his character was his moral courage—a quality which was equally apparent in his private and in his public life. With great geniality of disposition and a happy capacity for adapting himself to those about him, he combined a frankness so uncompromising that, at times, men who did not understand him might have been apt to think him aggressive. To those who did know him, on the other hand, his kindliness of heart was sufficient guarantee that this was not the case. No man did more in his time to bridge over the gulf that divided the two races, and his death created a gap in Native society which time alone could repair.

Besides Dwārikā Nāth Tagore, Rām Moni had two other sons, the younger of whom was Rama Nāth Tagore.

Rama Nath Tagore.

Rama Nāth Tagore (afterwards Maharaja Rama Nāth Tagore, C.S.I.), the third son of Rām Moni, was born in the year 1800, and was thus six years junior to his brother, Dwārikā Nāth, under whose auspices he entered on the business of life, and in most of whose public acts he was intimately associated.

Like Dwārikā Nāth, he studied English at Mr. Sherbourne's, where he was a schoolfellow of his cousin, the eminent Prosunna Coomar Tagore, learning Sanskrit, Bengali, and Persian at the same time under private tutors in his father's house.

After leaving school, he was placed for a time in the well-known firm of Alexander and Co., where he was initiated into the mysteries of commercial and banking business. When the Union Bank was started, in 1829, he was thus qualified to undertake the duties of treasurer, and was appointed to that responsible post through the influence of his brother. On the failure of the bank he acted as one of its liquidators, and gave great satisfaction to all who had dealings with him in that capacity.

Associated from an early age with Rām Mohun Roy, Rama Nāth became a convert to his theistic views, and, along with his brother and Prosunna Coomar Tagore, took a prominent part in the reforms initiated by him, and in the conduct of the affairs of the Brahma Sabha, of which he was made a trustee during the absence of Rām Mohun Roy in England.

From an early period of his life politics and political economy had a powerful interest for Rama Nāth, and he joined Prosunna

Coomar in starting the *Reformer*, a weekly newspaper in English, to be more particularly mentioned hereafter. He was at the same time a frequent contributor to the columns of the leading Anglo-Indian journals of the day, under the *nom de plume* of 'Hindoo.' At the great Free Press Dinner of 1835, already mentioned in connection with the career of Dwārikā Nāth Tagore, he, in the absence of his brother, responded to the toast of the 'People of India.' He was an energetic member of the Landholders' Society, and on its extinction took a leading part in the foundation of the British Indian Association, of which he was first a Vice-President, and subsequently President for the extended period of ten years.

'From the day of the Free Press Dinner,' says the writer of an obituary notice in the *Hindoo Patriot*, 'he was looked upon by both Natives and Europeans as a representative man There was scarcely a public meeting which he was not invited to address or preside over.'

In 1866 he was appointed a member of the Bengal Council, and by his independent and spirited advocacy of the rights of the agricultural community in that assembly, he acquired the title of the 'Ryot's Friend.'

Finance and political economy continued throughout his life to be his favourite studies, and largely occupied his pen. His activity as a political writer continued to an advanced age, and one of his latest works was an able pamphlet in which he exposed the mischief likely to result from the Rent Bill of 1859.

As a member of the Municipal Corporation of Calcutta, he was a persistent advocate of economy, and headed the party who, in the face of powerful opposition, 'made reform, retrenchment, and reduction of taxation their watchwords.' On the Burning Ghāt question he fought on the side of the people, and bore a large share in the task of raising the funds required to carry out the improvements in the ghāt which were ultimately decided on as the condition of its retention on the old site.

In 1873 he was appointed a member of the Legislative Council of the Governor-General and created a Raja.

During the famine of 1874 he was freely consulted by Lord Northbrook on the subject of the measures of relief that should be adopted, and, in recognition of his services in the matter, he was in the following year made a Companion of the Order of the Star of India.

On the occasion of the visit of the Prince of Wales to Calcutta, he was chosen by his countrymen to act as President of the Committee for the reception of His Royal Highness at the Belgatchia Villa. The excellence of the arrangements amply justified the choice, and Rama Nāth received a handsome ring from the Prince as a souvenir of the occasion.

At the durbar held to celebrate the assumption of the Imperial title by Her Majesty the Queen, Lord Lytton conferred on him the title of Maharaja.

Though not so wealthy a man as some

of the other leading members of the family, Rama Nāth was open-handed in his charities, public and private. 'There was not a public object,' says the writer quoted, 'which did not receive pecuniary help from him if an appeal was made to him. He was connected with almost all the public societies of Calcutta, literary, scientific, and charitable; his whole career was a career of public usefulness and benevolence.'

In disposition he was one of the most amiable of men: in his manners, while unassuming, he was frank and affable. He died on June 10, 1877, after a protracted illness.

A few months previously a movement, supported by the Chief Justice and some of the other Judges of the High Court, Mr. Schalch, Mr. Bullen Smith, and other leading members of society, had been set on foot for the purpose of voting him a suitable public memorial, but it was abandoned on account of his illness.

His death formed the occasion of the

following letter from Lord Lytton to the Honourable Rai Kristo Dass Pal Bahadur :—

'MY DEAR SIR,—I am deeply grieved to learn, by your letter to Colonel Burne, the sad news of the death of our friend the Maharaja Rama Nāth Tagore Bahadur. It is not merely a private loss, but I lament with you and the Maharaja's numerous friends to whom I beg you to express my sincere personal sympathy in their bereavement. By the Maharaja's death both the Government and the whole Native community of Bengal have lost a wise, an honest, and a trusted adviser, and by none who knew him is his loss deplored on public grounds more truly than by yours, my dear Sir,

'Always faithfully,
(Sd.) 'Lytton.'

DEVENDRA NATH TAGORE.

Babu Dwārikā Nāth Tagore left three sons, Devendra Nāth, Girendra Nāth, and Nogendra Nāth, the eldest of whom, Devendra Nāth Tagore, has, by his life of asceticism and devotion to religious meditation, acquired a high reputation for sanctity among the followers of Rām Mohun Roy, and the title of 'The Indian Hermit.'

He was born in 1818, and, after studying first at Rām Mohun Roy's school and subsequently at the Hindoo College, was placed for a time in his father's firm of Carr, Tagore, and Co., in order that he might qualify himself for commercial pursuits. Devendra Nāth's thoughts were, however, fixed on spiritual things, and when he was barely of age, he founded a society, called the *Tatwa Bodhini Sabha*, for the purposes of religious inquiry and discussion; but he afterwards joined the Brahma Samaj, and established a Brahma school in Calcutta. He was one of the original projectors of the *Indian Mirror*, which was edited in the first instance by Babu Man Mohan Ghose; and, on Babu Keshab Chandra Sen, who had succeeded that gentleman in the editorial chair, separating from the Samaj, he started the *National Paper*.

He was the first Brahmist to show the courage of his convictions by marrying his daughter according to the Brahmist rites and abandoning the use of the Brahminical thread.

Beyond acting for a time as Honorary Secretary to the British-Indian Association, he has taken little part in secular affairs and he at one time retired for some years to the Himalayas, for the purpose of religious meditation. He is, however, a voluminous writer on religious subjects, and is the author of a large number of treatises and tracts chiefly dealing with the tenets of Brahmism.

He has ~~five~~ sons, the second of whom is Satyendra Nāth Tagore, who was the first native of India to pass the competitive examination for the Indian Civil Service.

Though the career of Babu Dwārikā Nāth Tagore takes precedence of that of his distinguished relative, Prosunna Coomar, in order of time, he was a scion of the younger branch of the family.

Darpa Narayan and his Descendants.

To return to Darpa Narayan, the elder brother of Nilmoni. The wealth which he acquired, partly by commercial transactions and partly by service under the French Government at Chandernagore, enabled him to purchase, at a public sale for arrears of revenue, the immense property of Parganeh Ootter Seroorper. The lands which were included under this designation, and which formed part of the estates of the Rajas of Rājshahai, then in the hands of the well-known Rani Bhobani, covered an area of no less than 249 square miles. Such, however, was the state of the country at that period of British rule that they yielded to the landholders a net revenue of only Rs. 13,000 a year, and they fell to the bid of the fortunate Darpa Narayan for the sum of Rs. 91,500.

Darpa Narayan had seven sons, Radha Mohun, Gopee Mohun, Krishna Mohun, Hurry Mohun, Peary Mohun, Ladly Mohun, and Mohini Mohun.

The first and the third of these he disinherited for misconduct, giving them, however, Rs. 10,000 each for their subsistence. To Peary Mohun, who was deaf and dumb, he bequeathed Rs. 20,000, while the bulk of his enormous property was left in equal shares to Gopee Mohun, Hurry Mohun, Ladly Mohun, and Mohini Mohun.

Gopee Mohun Tagore.

Never did a splendid patrimony fall into worthier hands than the share of Darpa Narayan's property to which his second son, Gopee Mohun, thus succeeded.

In the extent, if not in the depth, of his scholarship, he fully maintained the reputation of his illustrious ancestry, adding to proficiency in Sanskrit, Persian, and Urdu a competent knowledge of English, French, and Portuguese. Like his father, he held an appointment under the French Government at Chandernagore, and he extended his already large estates by the purchase of landed properties in Rājshahai, Dinajpur,

Jessore, and other districts. As a proof of his immense wealth, it used to be said that he never sat without a lakh of rupees by his side; and, as a matter of fact, the jewelled *pāndān* (betel-box) and *hookah*, which he used in his *boytak-khāneh*, were alone worth that sum. What, however, is more to the purpose, he at one time lost twenty lakhs of rupees in opium transactions without being sensibly the poorer for it; and, when he died, he was in a position to bequeath to his six sons properties which gave each of them a handsome fortune.

Great as were his accumulations, he was nevertheless profuse in his private expenditure, liberal in his patronage of art, learning and religion, and lavish in his public charities. To pandits and ghātaks he was especially liberal, and on the occasion of a certain marriage in his family he is said to have presented several hundreds of the latter class, who attended the ceremony, with a hundred rupees apiece.

He appears to have possessed a strong passion for Hindoo music, proficients in which art were always sure of a liberal welcome from him. Performances were frequently held in his house, and two of the most famous professors of the day, Sajjoo Khan and Lāla Kewal Kishen, received regular monthly stipends from him. Nor was poetry forgotten by him. Kali Dass Mukerjea, the composer of many popular songs and hymns, surnamed Mirza, from his adoption of the Hindustani costume, and Lakhi Kanta, another well-known lyric poet of the day, were among his pensioners and constant attendants.

Among the great houses of Calcutta none was so famous as that of Gopee Mohun Tagore for the sumptuousness with which the Annual Durga Puja festival was celebrated in it. On such occasions the *élite* of European and Native society were among his guests. The Nawab of Chitpore, whose exclusiveness was proverbial, was an annual visitor at these entertainments, at which an enclosure in the spacious compound used to be set apart for him.

The well-known twelve *Sivas* and Temple to Kali, which form so conspicuous an object on the bank of the river Hughli at Mulajore, were erected by Gopee Mohun. During his lifetime all who resorted to them were liberally entertained at his expense, and large numbers of poor people are still daily fed there.

He earned a still higher title to the gratitude of posterity by the part he took in the foundation of the Hindoo College, to which he contributed largely. In consideration of their share in this work, he and the Maharaja of Burdwan were made hereditary Governors of the institution; and in the commemorative marble tablet set up in the Presidency College his name may be seen next to that of the Maharaja. The right of nominating a free student to the College was further conferred on him and his hereditary descendants, and one of the foundation scholarships was named, after him, the Gopee Mohun Tagore scholarship.

Gopee Mohun Tagore was a rigid Hindoo,

but he was capable on occasion of rising above superstitious prejudices unsanctioned by religion. Thus, when the celebrated painter, Chinnery, visited Calcutta, most of the Native nobility were deterred from having their portraits taken by the vulgar notion that the process would entail upon them a premature death. Gopee Mohun Tagore, however, showed himself superior to this idle apprehension, and, though his brothers all held back, consented to sit. The picture that was the result is still preserved as an heirloom in the family.

Gopee Mohun was noted for the geniality of his disposition, and was always ready to avail himself of an occasion for a joke. As an instance of this pleasing feature in his character, a story is told that, on a certain up-country pundit offering to stop by incantations a prolonged fall of rain, which threatened to interfere with the marriage procession of his two youngest sons, he promised to reward him liberally if he succeeded. The incantations were performed accordingly, but the rain continued unabated.

'How now, pundit?' said Gopee Mohun, 'in spite of your incantations, the rain is still falling as before.'

'Sir,' replied the Brahmin, 'I have undertaken to stop the rain falling from the clouds, but I cannot send back that which has already left them. When that has all fallen, the rain will cease.'

'The reward which you have not earned by your incantations,' said Gopee Mohun, 'you have merited by your wit;' and he gave him the stipulated present.

The following anecdote, still current in Calcutta and its vicinity, at once furnishes an example of his quickness at repartee and illustrates the light in which the Tagore family regard their position in Hindoo society.

A religious procession, headed by Raja Rāj Krishna, who, in his younger days, was somewhat lax in his observance of the rules of Hindooism, was passing the residence of Gopee Mohun. Finding the Raja barefooted, taking an active part in the ceremony, Gopee Mohun asked him good-humouredly how many parts he had played in his day. The Raja's reply was offensive, alluding as it did to the stain on the caste of the Tagore family. 'I have, no doubt, played many parts,' he said, 'but I have been unable to find you anywhere.'

'No wonder,' rejoined Gopee Mohun, drawing himself up and significantly adjusting his Brahminical thread, 'no wonder, Raja; I am where you cannot reach.'

As already remarked, Gopee Mohun Tagore was no less munificent in his private than in his public charities. One among many instances of his liberality to his dependents was his purchase of a valuable estate in the district of Rājshahai for the benefit of Ram Mohun Mookerjee, his dewan; while the assistance he rendered in the time of need to the father of Raja Baroda Kanta Rai, of Jessore, and to Babu Bishwa Nāth Chowdhuri, shows that his beneficence was not limited to those whose services constituted a claim upon him. The former was enabled by his assistance to bring to a successful issue a suit which threatened him with the loss of his ancestral property, a service which led to the establishment of the most intimate social relations between the two houses ; and the latter was maintained by him in comfort when in reduced circumstances.

Gopee Mohun left six sons, Soorjee Coomar, Chundra Coomar, Nunda Coomar, Kal Coomar, Huro Coomar, and Prosunna Coomar, two of whom, Huro and Prosunna, in their lives and their posterity, have added in a memorable degree to the lustre of the family name.

Soorjee Coomar, the eldest, displayed at an early age a marked aptitude for business, and, even during his father's lifetime, was entrusted with the management of his extensive estates. Both father and son were, however, in common with other capitalists of experience, outwitted by a needy adventurer of the name of Smith. This man had set on foot an extensive project for the construction of a dockyard with borrowed capital, and by his plausible representations secured the co-operation of the firm of Barretto and Co., who not only themselves advanced him six lakhs of rupees, but persuaded Gopee Mohun Tagore to come forward with a similar sum for the purposes of the undertaking. Soorjee Coomar was appointed Banian to the firm; but notwithstanding his circumspection the scheme speedily collapsed, involving both Gopee Mohun and Barretto in heavy loss.

Soorjee Coomar was also a large shareholder in the Commercial Bank, which was established about that time, and exercised a considerable influence in its management.

He died at the early age of thirty, without male issue, but leaving a grandson on his daughter's side, the well-known Raja Dakhina Ranjan Mukerjea, who subsequently became a Taluqdar of Oudh, and was for a long time secretary of the Oudh Taluqdars' Association.

Goopee Mohun's second son, Chundra Coomar Tagore, was well-known to the

European community of the time for the great and intelligent interest taken by him in public matters, and for his skill as a chess-player. He succeeded his father in the hereditary governorship of the Hindoo College. Unfortunately, however, he was of a speculative disposition, and so seriously involved the family estate by his ventures in the opium market as to render imperative the partition to be presently referred to.

Nundo Coomar and Kali Coomar mixed but little in public affairs, but were well-known for their generous dispositions, and Kali Coomar possessed a great reputation among his countrymen as an accomplished Urdu scholar.

Huro Coomar Tagore.

Huro Coomar's title to fame rests less on his public career than on his blameless life, his amiability of character and his eminence as a Sanskrit scholar. In common with his brother, Prosunna, and his second cousin, Dwārikā Nāth, he was a pupil in Mr.

Sherbourne's school Thence he was sent to the Hindoo College, in the foundation of which, as has just been seen, his father had taken so prominent a part.

There, aided by the private tuition of Mr. Anselm, the head-master, he made rapid progress in his studies, and became an accomplished Persian, as well as English, scholar.

His first Sanskrit teacher was, however, the Guru Mahashay, one Jhoro Guru, a Brahman and a native of Jessore, who had taught him his alphabet. This man's system of instruction, based on the Kalapa Byakarana, appears to have been of a more thorough character than that generally in vogue at the time. But it was not long before the pupil surpassed the master, and became an enthusiastic student of Sanskrit literature. So complete, indeed, was the mastery he obtained over the language, that he acquired the rare power of conversing in it with fluency, while his skill in composition was excelled by none of his contemporaries.

It is related that he and his brother,

Prosunna. having resolved to erect a tablet to the memory of their father at the temple at Mulajore, and offered a prize for the best set of verses in Sanskrit for inscription thereon, Huro Coomar sent in anonymously a set composed by himself. Among the competitors were many of the best Sanskrit scholars of the day, but the judges unanimously selected the anonymous composition for the prize, and Huro's verses were accordingly inscribed on the tablet, where they still bear testimony to his scholarship and poetical genius.

Huro Coomar's zeal for Sanskrit led him, in after years, to enter upon the study of the Vedantic system, which was regarded with disfavour by the strict Hindoos of those days, as subversive of orthodoxy. In connexion with this circumstance it is related that Huro Coomar's cousin, Wooma Nundun, meeting him one day at a wedding-party, expressed regret at learning that he had engaged in this new study. On Huro Coomar asking him his reason for this feeling, Wooma Nundun expressed a fear that, from being a staunch Hindoo, he might become a freethinker. Huro Coomar replied with a smile :—

'You should bear in mind, good cousin, that Vyasa, the father of the Vedanta philosophy, was also the author of our Puranas; yet, according to your theory, he should have been the greatest infidel of his time.'

Gopee Mohun's love of music was inherited by his son, and Huro not only patronised but practised the art, studying it under the well-known Kalawat Hassu Khan, and becoming an accomplished singer and performer on the sitar.

Though his tastes did not lead him to engage in public affairs, Huro Coomar, by his admirable management of his own estates, showed himself to be a man of great business capacity.

The family property was at first held jointly by all the brothers ; but, being led by information received from a trusted servant to suspect that it was being seriously mismanaged, Huro at once consulted with

Prosunna Coomar as to the course that should be adopted, and they came to the conclusion that a partition was necessary to save their shares from destruction. After some opposition they succeeded in their efforts for this purpose, and a partition was effected.

Huro Coomar found his share greatly encumbered and deteriorated, but by dint of thrift and good management he in time succeeded in not only restoring, but increasing it.

He died in the year 1858, leaving two sons, Jotendra Mohun Tagore and Sourendra Mohun Tagore, whose distinguished careers will be noticed hereafter, and a reputation for 'learning, ability, accomplished politeness, probity, and honourable feeling.'

Prosunna Coomar Tagore.

Of a very different type of character from his elder brother, Huro Coomar, was Gopee Mohun's youngest son, Prosunna Coomar Tagore. His equal in rectitude of character and in scholarship, his superior in breadth of culture, he possessed in the highest degree that political spirit and that taste for public life which the amiable Huro lacked.

Like Dwārikā Nath Tagore, he was essentially a man of action; like Dwārikā Nath, too, he was always ready to advance the cause of charity or progress. But his views were those of the statesman, rather than the mere philanthropist; and he added to forensic eloquence and a profound knowledge of English and Indian jurisprudence a degree of literary skill and ambition which placed him in the front rank of the native writers of his time. As a Member of the Governor-General's Legislative Council, he reached the highest pinnacle of political honour to which a Native could aspire, and one to which no Native before him had attained. In his triune capacity of lawyer, counsellor, and author, it is not too much to say, he was the most conspicuous man Bengal has yet produced, and one whose reputation was equally great among his own countrymen and among Europeans.

Prosunna Coomar Tagore was born in Calcutta on Monday, December 21, 1801, being thus seven years junior to Dwārikā Nāth. Like his brother, Huro Coomar, and, indeed, in company with him, he received the rudiments of education under the paternal roof, and was afterwards sent to the school of that Mr. Sherbourne who has already been more than once mentioned in these pages, and whose lot it was to impart the elements of English to so many of the distinguished Natives of the day.

Mr. Sherbourne taught at a house near what is now the Adi-Brahmo Samaj, in the Chitpore Road. Little seems to be known of him, except that he was the son of a Brahman mother and took great pride in his lineage; and, as a proof of the respect in which he was held by his old pupils, it is said that he was in the habit of receiving from the well-to-do among them the annual gifts (*pūjā bārsik*), which it is customary to offer to members of the twice-born caste.

From Mr. Sherbourne's school, as was

stated in the notice of Huro Coomar, Prasunna Coomar Tagore was transferred to the Hindoo College, where he continued his studies under Mr. Anselm. Unlike the great bulk of his fellow-countrymen in later days, however, he was not content to lay aside his books on completing his college curriculum, but continued his education diligently long after that period, engaging Mr. Halifax, Professor, of Mathematics in the College, to superintend his studies.

Prosunna Coomar may, in fact, be justly said to have been a diligent student all his life. Long before he entertained any idea of adopting the law as a profession, he had pursued its study as a pastime ; and, when twitted by an associate with the uselessness of such knowledge to a man of his wealth and position, he had replied that the mind was like a good housewife, who was sure to utilise, some time or other, everything she had in store.

His subsequent career was destined to furnish a striking illustration of the truth of this reflection ; for, having been induced, by heavy losses incurred in the course of business, to get himself enrolled as a pleader of the Sudder Court, he achieved so rapid a success as not only to recuperate, but to add largely to, his immense fortune. But he did more than this, and established a lasting title to the gratitude of the profession, which, from being a mere refuge for the needy— shunned, as degrading, by men of position— came, mainly by virtue of his efforts and example, to be looked upon as the most honourable and lucrative career, outside the service of Government, which a Native could follow. The cavalierly treatment, not altogether unjustified by the general calibre of the class, to which the too persevering pleader had hitherto been subjected by even the most amiable of Sudder judges, gave place in the presence of Prosunna Coomar, however much he might insist, to patient and respectful attention.

Such was the ability with which he conducted his cases that, on the death of Mr.

Baly, the Government pleader, he was nominated by the majority of the Court to succeed him, and, in spite of some opposition on the part of a minority of the judges and a member of the Board of Revenue, on the ground of his holding large landed property within the jurisdiction of the Court, the nomination was confirmed.

The success with which he discharged his duties in his new capacity established him in the confidence of the Government, and added largely to his professional reputation. 'To a profound knowledge of Indian law,' says the writer of an obituary memoir published in the columns of the *Hindoo Patriot* of August 31, 1868, 'Babu Prosunna Coomar united a hard common sense and keen sagacity which at once secured him the first position in the Bar. Urdu was then the Court language; but he was a first-rate Persian scholar and had therefore no difficulty in making himself heard. Master of real property law, he was unrivalled in that line, and his deep and painstaking researches into the manifold bearings of the Hindoo law made him also an authority on that subject. Unlike many of his brother pleaders, he was not only intimately acquainted with the substantive laws, but with their history from the earliest times. For the last four decades we may say he lived history. There was scarcely any important law, particularly relating to land, which was enacted during the last forty years, regarding which he was not consulted by the Government. But he was also familiar to a degree with the history of the prior Regulations and Acts. To us he appeared to be a walking library. Whenever we had doubts respecting the origin, history, or meaning of any laws, the moment we referred to him our doubts were solved.'

Some idea of the enormous practice he enjoyed may be formed from the fact stated by him in a letter addressed to the Registrar of the Court, in connexion with an application he had made for six months' leave of absence, that on a certain date in the year 1849 he held briefs in no fewer than ninety-six cases, of thirty-six of which he was in sole charge.

Though his professional income averaged little less than 20,000*l.* a year, he abandoned the Bar while still in the prime of life, to embark on that less restricted career to which his tastes and his ambitions clearly pointed. But he continued all his life to be freely consulted both by the Government and its officers and by private suitors, and was always ready to give those who applied to him the full benefit of his learning and advice, without looking for any other reward than the satisfaction derived from the act.

'In after life,' says a contemporary, 'he placed the mature fruit of his legal lore and vast experience at the service of his country, free of cost. There has not since been a single case of any importance in which his opinion was not sought, and in which it was not freely and most readily given. Indeed, no man had any confidence in his own case until he had the assurance of Babu Prosunna Coomar, and so great was the anxiety to get his opinion that people travelled hundreds of miles from the furthest parts of India for the purpose.'

To the extraordinary memory which, conjoined with extensive research, justified the description of Prosunna Coomar as 'a walking library,' there is abundant testimony from many different quarters. Not only 'the date of a particular Government letter; the number of a particular section of a particular law; the chapter and verse of some obscure old Smriti,' but 'the whole history of British administration in India, from the most important facts down to the smallest minutiæ' is said to have been at his fingers' ends.

The first instance in which we find Prosunna Coomar Tagore taking a leading part in any of the political movements of the day was on the occasion of the passing of Regulation III of 1828 by Lord William Bentinck's administration. This was one of a series of measures by which the Government, with but imperfect discrimination and inadequate regard for the interests of actual possessors, sought to repair the injury done to the Exchequer in past times by reckless or fraudulent alienations of revenue in the shape of grants of lakhiraj, or revenue free, tenures. The ostensible object of the Regulation was to expedite the adjudication of appeals from the decisions of the revenue authorities in regard to lands, or rents, occupied or collected by individuals without payment of Government revenue, by the appointment of special commissioners for the purpose. The feeling of the Lakhirajdars was that the real purpose of the measure was to transfer the trial of such appeals from an impartial tribunal to one which would be strongly biassed in favour of the Government; and to some extent there can be no doubt that this was its tendency.

The Regulation, moreover, contained several clauses obviously detrimental to the actual interests of the Lakhirajdars.

Against this enactment the three friends, Dwārikā Nāth Tagore, Prosunna Coomar Tagore, and Rām Mohun Roy, drew up and forwarded to the Court of Directors a powerful appeal. The protest was not successful, but the Court of Directors called upon the Local Government for an explanation of the grounds of the enactment, and the example set was one which was destined to bear useful fruit in the future.

The warning it conveyed was, however, so far unheeded or forgotten, that some ten years later, the Government, at the instance of the Board of Revenue, of which Mr. Ross Mangles was then secretary, was induced to engage in a wholesale crusade against the Lakhirajdars throughout Bengal. Resumption proceedings were set on foot simultaneously in every district, and the device, usual when high-handed action was to be sustained, of appointing special officers for the trial of the suits was resorted to.

These proceedings, as might have been expected, raised a storm of indignation all over the country, and after a period of fierce newspaper controversy, in which Prosunna Coomar Tagore, on the side of the Lakhiraj dars, and Mr. Ross Mangles on that of the Government, took leading parts, a great public meeting was convened at the Town Hall on November 30, 1839, by Babus Dwārikā Nāth, and Prosunna Coomar Tagore and others, who, as the founders and leaders of the Landholders' Society, had constituted themselves, and been recognised by the Government, as the representatives of the landed interest in Bengal.

Of this Society, which had been established in April 1838, and which continued to discharge most important functions till it gave place to the British-Indian Association in 1851, Prosunna Coomar Tagore and Mr. Cobb Hurry, at that time Editor of the *Englishman* newspaper, were the secretaries, and the respect its deliberations commanded must be attributed, in no small degree, to the influence which Prosunna Coomar exercised over them, and the ability and discretion with which he discharged the duties of his secretaryship.

The meeting of 1839 was so largely

attended, and created so much excitement in the community, that the Government was led to adopt extraordinary precautions for the preservation of the peace. It is needless to say there was nothing either in the proceedings, or in the temper of the large concourse of people, both Europeans and Natives, whom it drew together, to justify any such anxiety.

After the Report of the Committee of the Landowners' Society, drawn up by Mr. Cobb, Hurry and Babu Prosunna Coomar Tagore, had been read and adopted, the meeting was addressed at length by Mr. Dickens, Mr. Turton, Babu Dwārikā Nāth Tagore, Mr. Leith, Mr. W. F. Fergusson, Mr. Hume, and others, and a series of resolutions were adopted, the most important of which was:— 'That in the present state of the question of resumption of rent-free tenures, and with reference to Mr. Secretary J. E. Grant's letter of November 25, it is expedient to appeal to the authorities in England with the view to obtain complete redress.'

The final result of the agitation was that

Circular Orders were issued by the Board of Revenue, so far modifying the obnoxious law as to exempt from its operation religious endowments, lands held rent-free since 1790, and parcels of land of not more than fifty bighahs in a single village.

Prosunna Coomar's first literary enterprise was the foundation, in conjunction with his friend and relative, Rama Nāth Tagore, of a weekly newspaper in the English language, called *The Reformer*. The writer of the obituary in the *Hindoo Patriot*, already referred to, speaks of him as having started this paper when scarcely out of his teens. This, however, is not literally correct, the first number of *The Reformer* having made its appearance in 1831, when Prosunna Coomar was just thirty years of age.

His object in embarking in the enterprise appears to have been of a purely political nature—the advocacy of Native rights, which had just then been so rudely assailed; and *The Reformer*, while it lasted, did valuable service in this direction. A large share in its conduct was taken by Mr. Crowe, a gentleman of European parentage and of conspicuous ability, who was engaged by the proprietors for the purpose.

Mr. Crowe's own career was a remarkable one, and furnishes a striking instance of a young man surmounting by sheer application the disadvantages arising from the absence of even the most rudimentary education during the period of life usually devoted to school. Brought up at Patna from early infancy by a widowed mother who spoiled him, he reached the age of sixteen not only without learning to read or write, but unacquainted with any language but Hindustani. Being taken one day by his mother to the district court, where she was engaged in a law-suit, he happened to attract the attention of the presiding magistrate, who reproached him with his ignorance, with the result of so shaming him that he persuaded his mother to take him down to Calcutta, and send him to school.

Arriving in Calcutta in 1822, he shortly

after became a pupil of the well-known Mr. Drummond, who then occupied the site of what afterwards became the **Anunda Bazar** in Dhurmtolah Street.

There, in spite of many obstacles, not the least among them being the persecution to which he was subjected at the hands of his more fortunate schoolmates, he applied himself so diligently and perseveringly to his studies that, when he left the school three years later, he was able to obtain employment in the Quartermaster-General's office on the comparatively handsome salary of a hundred rupees a month.

So meritorious were his services in this position that in 1830 he obtained the post of head clerk to the Board of Revenue. At the same time he developed a strong talent for literary pursuits, and was a valued contributor to many of the journals of the day. Subsequently he obtained an appointment as deputy-collector and surveyor, in which capacity he continued to serve the Government with credit and distinction, till his death in 1847.

Prosunna Coomar Tagore early discovered Mr. Crowe's merits and ability, and was his staunch friend throughout his career.

In connexion with *The Reformer* Prosunna Coomar also carried on for some time a Bengali paper, called the *Unnobadak*, containing translations of articles from it.

At an early age Prosunna Coomar came under the influence of Rām Mohun Roy; and, as in the case of Dwārikā Nāth Tagore, the consequence was a radical change in the religious views in which he had been brought up. Like his father, Gopee Mohun, and his brother, Huro Coomar, he was in his youth a strict Hindoo, and performed the customary *puja* daily, in company with the latter. His conversion to the theistic views of his friend was the result of no blind admiration of the genius of the reformer, still less of recklessness or a love of novelty, but the outcome of patient and conscientious investigation, prompted by the love of truth alone. Once convinced, he threw his whole soul into the cause of what he believed to be the truth, and among his earliest literary efforts was a pamphlet entitled 'An appeal to his countrymen, by Prosunna Coomar Tagore,' in which he upheld in powerful language the worship of one God.

But, though unable any longer to subscribe personally to the tenets of modern Hindooism, he never ceased to entertain for it that respect which every man of good feeling must retain for the faith of his ancestry and kindred. Nor did he consider it inconsistent with the demands of his new belief to dedicate the silver cot in which his venerated mother had slept, to the service of the family temple at Mulajore, where, towards the close of his life, he had it converted into a throne for the god, thus taking the most effectual step that could be devised for its permanent preservation.

Prosunna Coomar Tagore always evinced a lively interest in the education of his countrymen. On the death of his brother, Chunder Coomar, he succeeded to one of the two Governorships of the Hindoo College, hereditary in his family; and as early as the year 1841 we find him taking a conspicuous part in the settlement of a scheme of Regulations for the schools and colleges under the General Committee of Public Instruction.

The minute which he recorded on the subject, and which was published by the Government along with the Regulations in question, shows how clear an insight he possessed into the educational needs of his countrymen. On the importance of vernacular schools he laid hardly less stress than the most advanced reformers of the present day, remarking that, unlike the English seminaries, which were limited in their scope to a particular section of the community, they had a national object in view. This minute shows, further, how thoroughly he was convinced that the only chance of imparting Western ideas to the mass of the people of India, lay in including a sound vernacular education in the curriculum of the higher English seminaries.

'The people in general,' he remarked, 'have a natural thirst after learning, but we are unprovided at present either with the necessary works for the purposes of tuition, or with competent teachers. Could we but find a few Native youths qualified in the English arts and sciences, and possessed of sufficient knowledge to express their newly-acquired ideas through the vernacular language, they might, we think, be trained in the combined duties of authors and teachers. This were, at least, the first and safest step eventually to establish a permanent system of Indian national education.'

With this view he prepared an elaborate scheme, including arrangements for a certain amount of instruction in Sanskrit, for the improvement of vernacular education in the institutions in question, and drew up a list of appropriate books for use in connexion with it.

Had this, or some similar scheme, been persistently adhered to during the forty years that have intervened between that time and the present, the means available to-day for carrying out a useful system of mass education would probably have left very little to be desired.

When, during the administration of Lord Dalhousie, it was proposed to reorganise the establishment of the Hindoo College and erect the higher English branch into a separate institution, under the title of the Presidency College, Prosunna Coomar Tagore subordinated all considerations of family pride to the wishes of the Government, and, together with his brother, Huro Coomar, surrendered his hereditary rights and privileges into its hands.

That it was only after a painful conflict of feeling that he brought himself to make this surrender is not to be wondered at, and it is impossible not to sympathise with the sense of just indignation at the high-handed action of the authorities of the day, which finds expression in the following passage in one of the letters on the subject written by him to Mr. Mouatt, then Secretary of the Council of Education: 'Lest my silence should be construed into concurrence, I shall avail myself of the circumstance of the document' (the draft of the Government letter) 'having been officially communicated to me, to place on record my protest against the radical change of the constitution of the College which is now contemplated.

'I cannot, however, refrain on this occasion from expressing my feelings of regret and mortification with regard to a plan which, as it appears to me, is designed, by throwing open the College to all classes of students, not only to change its exclusive character to the entire subversion of the original intentions of its founders, but as much as possible to obliterate their names and consign to oblivion the memory of their efforts for the advancement of knowledge. Such being the case, I, as a representative of one of the hereditary Governors of the Institution, apart from the consideration of the competency of the parties to give effect to such proposal, or my personal opinion as to the exclusive character of the College, cannot but feel mortified to find that after the College had been founded by my father in conjunction with other public-spirited Natives by private subscription, and by the subsequent accession of aid from Government had continued upwards of thirty-five years on its original plan and reached its present condition, during which long period the hereditary rights of the Governors were solemnly acknowledged by successive Governments, the Council of Education should now, instead of adopting measures to preserve the efforts of the founders in the grateful recollection of succeeding generations, have directed their attention to the opposite end, and, though it is proposed that the descendants of those who have an hereditary right in the management of the College should forego that privilege for the equivocal advantage of a seat in the Council of Education, no man who has any feeling of respect for his ancestors could with satisfaction join a constitution modelled on such principles. I trust I shall not be placed in a situation so painful as to be under the necessity of declining the offer.'

This was outspoken, but it was not uncalled for.

On receipt of the final orders of the Bengal

Government, Prosunna Coomar and his brother chose the alternative of surrendering all their rights absolutely to the Government rather than become consenting parties to a measure for revolutionising the College, at the same time urging the claims of the founders to some such memorial in the new Institution as might perpetuate the memory of their connexion with it.

In accepting the offer of the brothers, Lord Dalhousie recorded a minute expressive of his hope that the public spirit of the original founders might be permanently commemorated by the erection of a suitable memorial in the new Presidency College. But, although the Governor of Bengal assented to the justice and propriety of this proposal, it was left to the present head of the family, the Honourable Maharaja Jotendra Mohun Tagore, after a lapse of a quarter of a century, to carry it into effect by the erection at his own expense of a tablet, with a suitable inscription, in the College.

Though an advocate of the education of Native females under certain circumstances,

Prosunna Coomar was opposed to the establishment of public schools for the purpose. His views on the subject find full expression in a letter addressed by him to Mr. F. J. Halliday, in connexion with a proposal of Lord Dalhousie to adopt as his own the school founded by Mr. Bethune. Native society, he pointed out, was divided, like that of other civilised countries, into the higher, the middle, and the lower class. Among the first a taste for European knowledge was confined to a few the majority of the elder portion being still wholly indifferent to it. Even the enlightened minority were averse to sending their female children or wards to a public school, where they would have to associate with those of a lower social grade. The usage of the country and religious precept, again, made it essential that girls of good family should be married before the age of ten, at the latest, and if a girl were sent to a public school at six years of age, she could remain there as a pupil only three or four years, which would be in sufficient to admit of her completing her studies. The little education she might take with her from school would be forgotten in the midst of domestic enjoyment, or, it might be, in a family where female education was not appreciated. As to the middle class, though, on the whole, they were better educated than the higher classes, their thirst for knowledge was the result of worldly motives, rather than of a desire to improve themselves. But no such motive would come into play in the case of female education. The lower classes, on the other hand, might, no doubt, be induced by pecuniary temptations to send their daughters to school; but their presence would deter the middle class from encouraging the movement.

With the exception of the 'Appeal' above mentioned, the separate published writings of Prosunna Coomar Tagore were all on subjects of Indian law. They are distinguished by a purity and lucidity of style which, for a foreigner writing in so difficult a language as English, are remarkable; by extensive research, and by great logical acumen.

The earliest is 'A Concise Dissertation on certain points of the Hindoo Law, according to the Doctrine of the Mitacshara; the most important, the 'Vivada Chintamoni,' a translation from the Sanskrit of the commentary of Vachaspati Misra on the Hindoo law prevalent in Mithila, with a learned preface by the translator.

The 'Dissertation,' which was published in 1847, was suggested by the adverse decision of the Sudder Court in the famous Ramnuggur Appeal Case, in which the writer appeared on behalf of the Government, who claimed the right to succeed to the Ramnuggur Raj in the absence of legitimate heirs. The appellate court, in confirmation of the decision of the lower court, ruled that a claimant who held his pretension of heritable right in the sixth degree of the descending generation from the seventh of the ascending common ancestor, was entitled to the estate of a deceased proprietor according to the Mithila school of Hindoo law; and the object of the 'Dissertation' is to investigate the precise intent and meaning of the law, as prescribed in the 'Mitacshara' (which the writer held to be applicable to the claimant's case) with respect to Sapinda for inheritance, both in the ascending degree and in the descending generation.

The 'Vivada Chintamoni' was published in 1863 and dedicated to Sir Barnes Peacock then Chief Justice of the High Court of Calcutta.

In the preface the translator has given us a most learned and interesting dissertation on the development of the existing systems of Hindoo law; on the origin and position of the four great castes; and on the authority and authenticity of the Code of Menu and other cognate matters.

It contains an able and not unsuccessful vindication of the Brahmans against the charges of avarice, arrogance and ignorance brought against them by various writers. Contrasting the Christian priesthood with the Brahmans, who, he points out, are not a priesthood, he says : 'The former profess to be the successors of teachers who disclaimed wealth power, and even honour, and only required such a competency as should leave them free to attend to the duties of religion and the instruction of their flocks. They are expected to be versed in their sacred literature, and are in general amply provided for by the State, often by voluntary contributions, and style themselves or admit the style of reverend or even lord, in contempt of the most positive injunctions of the author of their religion. The latter are clothed with a sacred origin, and thereby entitled to the highest rank and supreme reverence; they are almost limited to learning as a profession, but no provision is made even for their absolute wants. They neither possess temporal power, nor arrogate the disposal of earthly kingdoms. They are altogether dependent for their subsistence on voluntary gifts, and are not even at liberty to receive them from the inferior classes —among whom, in the present day, are included some of the wealthiest men—or to act indiscriminately as priests without forfeiting their position in the opinion of their brethren as well as that of the laity.

'This comparison is made with a view, not to the reprobation of the habits or practices of the clergy of Europe, but to the exculpation of the Brahmans of India. They are, of all sacerdotal classes in the world, the most unassuming and the least grasping. At any rate, they have neither *aimed* at greater wealth, honour, or power than the sacred law has allowed, nor actually *gained* so much as they were entitled to by its decrees. It is asserted in works of authority, in which accuracy should be studied, that *Brahmans* " have maintained a more extensive sway than the priests of any other nation." Could these authors have forgotten to compare the commands of the author of the Christian religion with the history of the Papacy, or the position of the Prince Bishops of Germany and the Lord Bishops of England and France, to say nothing of those of Italy and Spain, or even the *bénéficiaires* of most of the European States, with incomes a thousand times larger than any Brahman ever enjoyed, under the most liberal or most bigoted princes of this continent?'

Apart from all question of its merits as a statement of facts and opinions, the discriminating reader must, we think, be struck by the elegance of style, the idiomatic ease, and the remarkable accuracy and purity of diction which distinguish the above passage, an elegance, an ease, an accuracy, and a purity which might be envied by many an English writer of repute, and which, in a foreigner, may well excite surprise. Yet the passage is in no respect an unfair example of the writer's literary skill. Look where one may in his published compositions, they are characterised by the same qualities, and the most acute critic would search in vain for any indication that they were not the productions of a highly-cultivated Englishman.

Prosunna Coomar's other works were the 'Table of Succession according to the Hindoo Law of Bengal,' 'the Rights of Bundhoos' (cognate kindred) 'according to the Western

School,' the 'Neum-patra, or Zemindaree Guide,' in Bengalee, and a series of short essays on various legal subjects published under the title of 'Loose Papers.'

It was in the latter end of 1850 that Prosunna Coomar resigned his office of pleader in the Sudder Court, and in the early part of November of the same year he left Calcutta on a tour in Assam, one of his objects, as described in a letter to Mr. F. A. E. Dalrymple, C.S., announcing his approaching departure, being to penetrate into the interior of that country, and examine the manners and customs of the wild tribes dispersed over it.

He appears, from an examination of his letter book of that year, to have returned to Calcutta in the beginning of June following. An account of his travels from his own hand would have been interesting; but unfortunately no letters on the subject seem to have been preserved.

About this time he appears to have entertained some intention of paying a visit to

England; but, finding no fellow-countryman of his own class willing to accompany him across the 'black water,' he had to abandon it.

In the beginning of 1853, however, he set out on a tour in Upper India, and extended his travels as far as Cashmere, which country he describes in a letter written to Prosunna Nāth Rae, after his return in the following September, as the paradise of the world in all respects but the habits and manners of its people and the character of its ruler.

During his stay there, which lasted twenty-five days, he paid a visit to the Maharaja at his request, on the express understanding that there was to be no interchange of complimentary gifts. At parting he presented His Highness with a telescope, remarking that he had nothing to give worthy of acceptance; but as a telescope brought distant objects near, he had decided on presenting him with one, in order that it might bring him sometimes to His Highness's memory.

In the year 1854 Prosunna Coomar was invited by the Governor-General, Lord Dalhousie, to undertake the office of Clerk Assistant to the Legislative Council, then newly-constituted under the Presidentship of that nobleman. Though the acceptance of the post must have involved considerable personal sacrifice, he gladly obeyed the summons, and his long familiarity with the laws of the country and their practical operation, enabled him to render in that capacity services of a kind which probably no other man, European or Native, could have done.

The drafts of the laws submitted by the Indian Law Commission in 1837, and afterwards referred to a Royal Commission in London, were returned to the Legislative Council in the year 1856, during his tenure of office; and the Committee of the Council, presided over by Sir Barnes Peacock, in presenting their first report on the subject, acknowledged in the most handsome terms ' the great assistance they had derived from his extensive knowledge and experience,' and his 'indefatigable exertions in carrying out their views.'

He also rendered the committee valuable assistance in the final revision of the Penal Code, and was one of a number of Oriental scholars chosen to examine and correct its translation into the vernacular of Bengal.

In 1851, the old Landowners' Society having ceased to exist, Prosunna Coomar, in conjunction with Rama Nāth Tagore and other leading members of Bengalee society, founded the existing British-Indian Association on a wider basis. Up to the time of his death Prosunna Coomar was one of its most active members, and he was largely instrumental in raising it to the position of influence which it still maintains.

Up to the time of his accepting the Clerk Assistantship to the Legislative Council he was a leading member of the committee, and although his official connexion with the Association then necessarily ceased for a time, he continued to be consulted on all occasions of importance and to give it the fullest benefit of his counsel. He, moreover, subscribed the princely sum of ten thousand rupees towards giving it a permanent habitation, and, on the death of the venerable Sir Radha Kanta Deb Bahadur, he was elected its President and continued to act in that capacity till his death.

While Prosunna Coomar Tagore filled the post of Clerk Assistant to the Council, his time seems to have been very fully occupied with his official labours, and more especially with the new Penal Code, which engaged much of the attention of the Committee of the Council.

From this period up to the time of the Mutiny, he seems to have resided continually in Calcutta. His opinions regarding the great crisis of 1857, a crisis during which his faith in the ultimate triumph of the British Government never for a moment wavered, possess a special interest.

The following passage from a letter written by him to Mr. F. A. E. Dalrymple, on May 5, 1856, shows how sinister at that date was the feeling among the Mahommedan portion of the community in connexion with the recent annexation of Oudh : ' We expect the ex-King of Lucknow by next week. He has taken Dwārikā Nāth's garden house for his residence. I doubt much if he will have the courage to go to England, as he will have to brave the sea sickness and the boisterous waves. I hear from Outram that even a trip on the Goomtee was a source of alarm to his Majesty.

' The followers of the Prophet say : " Look at the effects of injustice and the visitation of the prophet—that Lord Dalhousie fell sick ; Outram is the same ; Hayes is about to resign ; Sleeman is gone away on account of bad health ; General Low, who was formerly at Lucknow, and took a share in the annexation ——[1] Do not all these concurrent circumstances prove the truth of the visitation of the Prophet? " Lord Canning will neither visit the ex-King, nor receive his visit.'

---

[1] Something is apparently omitted here

On June 12, 1857, we find him writing to General Low, the Military Member of Council.

'MY DEAR GENERAL LOW,—There is a prophecy in Persian in which the Seikhs and Mahommedans of the North-West Provinces have implicit belief. I send you, with an abstract translation, an extract from it, which I find is in circulation in those parts, and has lately come into possession of the Mahommedans hereabouts, and of which copies are taken by them and read at their social meetings.

'You will perceive from this paper that they reckon the rule of the English at a hundred years; and, taking the rise of it from the Battle of Plassy, this is the month which completes that period. This circumstance influences the ignorant and credulous to rise in arms, and is the cause of both Hindoos and Mahommedans of those provinces uniting together. The Hindoos, including the Seikhs, have as much faith in the fakeers as the Mahommedans, as you are well aware.

'As you will readily understand that such papers must exercise a very powerful effect on the minds of Mahommedans in these parts, I have thought proper to communicate it to you.

Niamatoolla Wullee, a fakeer of the Panjaub, published a prophecy in Persian verse, to the number of thirty-eight couplets, in the year of the Hegira 570, or A.D. 1175.

'The author, after giving the succession of the Emperors of Hindustan from Timur to Nadir, and declaring that the latter would be succeeded by a powerful king, prophesies that the Seikhs would be in the ascendant for forty years. The Nazarenes were then to rule the country for a hundred years. A king from the west would then contend with the Christians, and great slaughter would take place, resulting in his success and the overthrow of his opponent. His reign was to be for forty years. Djezzal, who is represented in the Koran as to come to destroy unbelievers about the end of the world, was then to appear, followed first by Jesus, and then by Mehdee, as is also foretold in the Koran, to effect the destruction of Djezzal. The prophecy concludes by declaring the sovereignty of the followers of Jesus in the East would be at an end in 1280 Hegira, or A.D. 1864.'

He appears to have been strongly of opinion that the people of the North-Western Provinces would have shown no sympathy with the movement if the land in that part of the country had been settled permanently with the zemindars, as in Bengal. Thus, in a letter to Mr. Dalrymple, dated July 10, 1857, he writes :—

'You see the people have in many places joined with the mutineers. Would such a thing have happened had the Zemindary system been introduced there? There every ryot is a poor cultivator, having no capital to lose and no interest in the soil, and is entirely dependent on the village banker. This year the cultivation will be necessarily neglected, and with them the village bankers will become insolvent. The ryots have no alternative but to live on the plunder of their neighbouring villages, and the village bankers are the receivers of the ill-gotten property. But in Bengal, in a well-regulated Zemindary where the ryots are attached to the lord of the soil, could they have risen against the will of the Zemindar whose interest is identical with the interest of the British Government under the permanent settlement? If there be any symptom of a rise among any class in any Zemindary, and the Zemindar throw his turban before them, would they ever desert him? I have spoken in this way to the members of Government, and they seem to feel the force of my arguments. I hope, at the next settlement of the North-West Provinces, Lord Wellesley's promise of a permanent settlement on the Zemindaree system will be redeemed.'

He seems also to have regarded our maintenance of the independent Native States as an error of policy.

'The great mistake of Akbar,' he remarks (also in a letter to Mr. Dalrymple, written in the autumn of 1857), 'was that, when he conquered a country, he reinstated its sovereign as a tributary, thinking that gratitude would make him faithful. But after his death, as the Government became weak, these princes invariably shook off the yoke, and hence so many petty Rajpoot and other States. Our mistake was not to conquer many States, but to keep them in subjection and alliance, with the same view and expectation of gratitude. The result we see now.'

His correspondence shows him to have been throughout this time a warm admirer of the policy of Lord Canning, and he was one of the foremost in getting up the loyal demonstrations of 1857, and in the presentation of the address of confidence to that nobleman.

In the spring of 1858 an attack of facial paralysis obliged Prosunna Coomar to take six months' leave from his arduous duties of Clerk Assistant to the Council, and seek change of air. He did not start, however, till the opening of the river in July, on the 21st of which month he left Calcutta, in his own private pinnace, for Monghyr. There he staid in his own house, prettily situated at Peer Pahar till November, in the early part of which month he returned to Calcutta, much recruited in health.

On December 20, 1859, he again left Calcutta on a tour to Rangpur and Assam, in the steamer *Karatoya*, which he had lately had built, and did not return till the following July.

In the year 1861 Prosunna Coomar was made a member of the newly-constituted Municipal Commission, and an Honorary Magistrate, and in the beginning of the following year he was appointed a member of the Council of the Lieutenant-Governor of Bengal, in the proceedings of which body he took an active part whenever his health permitted him to attend the meetings.

He took an early opportunity to bring in a Bill, drafted by himself, for the Registration of Hindoo Wills and Powers of Adoption, which was, however, thrown out on a division on technical grounds.

Among the many subjects on which Pabu Prosunna Coomar Tagore was consulted by the Government or its officers, was the question of the comparative salaries which should be allowed to Europeans and Natives holding similar appointments and discharging similar duties, a question which had presented itself for consideration in connexion with the general scheme of the revision of official salaries, then under preparation by Mr. Ricketts.

Prosunna Coomar was of opinion that there ought, on principle, to be no difference in the salaries of members of the two races so circumstanced.

'The Government should not, for the sake of colour, or caste, or any other personal consideration,' he urged in a letter to Mr. Ricketts, 'expend the public revenue in unequal proportion among officers of equal responsibility; and even if one of these officers possess superior qualifications in any particular branch of knowledge not actually required for the discharge of his duties, the State should not, in consideration thereof, subject the public fund to any additional charge. The State should look to the capacity of persons for office and fix certain salaries as remuneration for the performance thereof; and whoever is found qualified in all respects for the post is entitled to such allowance, but the salaries should not vary with reference to difference of complexion or place of birth of the person holding office.

'On the other hand, it is alleged that the circumstances of the country should not be overlooked. Regarding this country as a dependency of Great Britain, the rulers would probably, from other considerations than the general principles above adverted to, wish to see Europeans holding the larger portion of the more important public offices. The advocates of the system of distinction between European and Native officers urge that persons of the former class cannot come to the country or live in it but at a considerable personal expense, to which the Natives are not liable; that they also run much risk in serving in climates not congenial to their constitutions, and that it is therefore fit that they should be compensated by receiving a higher rate of salary, and being allowed to return to their native land after a moderate period of service, on suitable retiring allowances. These are confessedly arguments founded on personal and relative considerations, and admissible on the score of expediency only. It is, however, a maxim with politicians that measures not founded on sound principle are of limited duration, as well as troublesome in their operation, and will consequently soon be changed for others. Hence, if the arrangement in contemplation be intended to be lasting in duration, and beneficial in the working, it is advisable to resort to sound principle, instead of being guided by feelings and prepossessions.'

Prosunna Coomar was not only a liberal patron of education, but was always ready to encourage literary merit. The 'Dayabhaga,' with commentaries, and the 'Dattaka Siromoni,' edited by Bharut Chunder Siromoni; the 'Badi-Bibada-Bhanjana,' by Pundit Broja Nath Bidyaratna, and the 'Krishv Sangraba,' by Grish Chunder Bidyaratna, were all brought out under his auspices and with his aid.

The first attempt on the part of Natives of Bengal to produce anything in the shape of a dramatic representation beyond the old Hindoo 'Jattra,' was due to his efforts. In his garden at Sura, with the assistance of a number of friends who had been his fellow-students at the Hindoo College, and others, he organised an amateur theatre, where Wilson's English version of the 'Utter Ram Charita' and Shakespeare's 'Merchant of Venice' were performed to large audiences. among whom were many distinguished Europeans.

He held strong opinions regarding the importance of the Sanskrit language as a means of enriching the vernacular, and fitting it to become the vehicle of Western scientific knowledge. As has been already seen, he advocated the introduction of Sanskrit studies even into the higher English schools, and he himself endowed a purely Sanskrit school at Mulajore in connexion with the family temple, where rhetoric, Nyaya philosophy, and Smriti are still taught on the system prevailing in the Bengal Toles, and some forty students are assisted with monthly stipends.

In his charities he was at once liberal and discriminating. Upwards of a hundred poor people, including many schoolboys, were fed daily at his house, and his annual gifts to learned pundits at the time of the great Dusserah festival exceeded those of any of his contemporaries. Among the numerous public institutions of a benevolent character befriended by him were the Chandny Hospital, of which he was a Governor, and the Garhanhatta Dispensary, of which he was long the mainstay.

What he gave publicly affords, however, but an imperfect measure of his expenditure on good works. The number of private recipients of his bounty, whether in the shape of annual allowances, or of occasional help in the hour of need, was legion, and included many poor Christians as well as Natives.

Among prominent instances of Prosunna Coomar's public spirit were his erection, at Patharia Ghatta, of the handsome and commodious bathing ghāt, designed especially for the convenience of respectable females, which forms so conspicuous a feature in the riparian architecture of Calcutta; his determined and successful opposition to the attempt of the Government to appropriate to its own uses the Strand bank lands, made over by his ancestors and others conditionally for the benefit of the town, and the works which, at great cost and in the face of immense natural difficulties, he carried out with the view of rendering the River Karatoya, which flowed through his estates in the Bogra district, navigable for laden country boats. Both in the matter of the erection of the Patharia Ghatta Ghāt, and in that of the construction and maintenance of the Karatoya works, he had to contend against an amount of official obstruction and pettifogging contentiousness which would have quenched the ardour of any less determined man.

He sat on the committee appointed under the Presidentship of Mr. Seaton-Karr to revise the municipal constitution of Calcutta, the report of which formed the basis of Act VI of 1863. As a member of the Corporation, he rendered the most valuable services on the finance committee, and, along with Maharaja Rama Nāth Tagore and Babu Rām Gopal Ghose, earned the thanks of the Hindoo community by his strenuous opposition to the removal of the Burning Ghāt. When, in the end, it was decided that the ghāt should remain where it stood, on the condition of its being remodelled upon a plan consistent with the requirements of sanitation and decency, he was largely instrumental in raising the necessary funds for the purpose.

In his private, as in his public, life Prosunna Coomar's bearing was marked by an absence of ostentation as rare among Natives of India of his wealth and social position as it was characteristic of the man. When he visited his estates, he, much to the astonishment and probably the disappointment of his tenants, travelled in a common wooden palanquin, such as one of his own Amlah, or any ordinary traveller, might have used; and when a number of his tenants, being told by him in answer to their inquiries on the subject, that he could not afford a silver palanquin, subscribed together the sum necessary for the purchase of such a luxurious equipage, he insisted on their taking back their money, remarking that a silver palanquin would be less convenient for his purpose than a wooden one.

Prosunna Coomar paid the common penalty of well-known public benefactors. The beggar, official as well as private, was ever at his gate. But he knew how to refuse when the object was of doubtful merit. Thus, when the Magistrate of Hughli applied to him for a subscription in aid of a road from Bidyabati to the shrine at Tarkessur, for the accommodation of pilgrims, he very properly replied:—

'Sir,—I am favoured with your letter inviting subscriptions for a road from Bidyabati to Tarkessur for the convenience of pilgrims.

'You are no doubt aware that the temple at Tarkessur yields large profits to its owner, or Mohunt, derived from the endowments attached to it and the offerings of the pilgrims. To facilitate access to the temple, in the manner you propose, would therefore be an encouragement to many to flock to it at all seasons of the year, and thereby promote the profits of the owner.

'Were the party himself to set such a plan on foot, no person could blame him for taking care of his interests; but no man, on public grounds, could justify any assistance being given to the project exclusively for the accommodation o pilgrims who may resort to the shrine, when the annual income of the temple is more than sufficient to carry the contemplated object into effect.

'To make the road in question by public subscription would, in fact, be for the benefit of the Mohunt of the temple, who should be called upon primarily to contribute for the purpose.

'Taking this view of the matter, it is questionable whether one-half of the expense of the road should be contributed by the Government from the general revenue. It is true that all improvements in the means of communication must be beneficial in the end; but in this instance the Government, as well as those private persons who contribute, will be encouraging at their expense the improvemen of the resources of the Mohunt, or owner of the temple.

'I trust that the motive which has led you to promote this work will induce you to reconsider the matter, after making such local inquiries as may be necessary to show the real state of things.'

Prosunna Coomar was always scrupulously exact in even the smallest matters of business. The discharge of an obligation, however trifling in itself, was in his eyes a sacred duty, from which he never willingly allowed himself to be excused.

On one occasion, when a friend at Bhāgalpur, whom he had commissioned to procure him some specially fine tobacco, declined to receive payment for it, he wrote: 'According to the rules of etiquette, if you persist, I shall be obliged to comply with your wishes; but it will prevent me from asking you for your kind assistance on future occasions, should I require anything from Bhāgalpur.'

The following letter to the Hon'ble Ashley Eden, then Secretary to the Government of Bengal, is interesting, not only as embodying an expression of Prosunna Coomar's opinion on the special question dealt with in it, but as showing the view he took of the proper attitude of the Government in respect of projects of reform which, however desirable in themselves, are in advance of Native opinion:—

'MY DEAR SIR,—I have the pleasure to acknowledge the receipt of your favour of the 11th instant, enclosing a copy of a correspondence on the subject of the Hindoo practice of taking sick people to the river-side to die and requesting me to submit to His Honour the Lieutenant-Governor my opinion on the following points:—

'(1) Whether the practice of taking the

sick to the river-side prevails, and to what extent?

'(2) Whether there is reason to believe that it is used as a means of getting rid of persons who are obnoxious or troublesome to their relations?

'(3) Whether the dread of exclusion from caste, and the belief in the efficacy of a river-side death, act as inducements to the destruction of life in the case of those who are taken to the river-side to die?

'(4) Whether the prohibition of the practice would be distasteful to the intelligent portion of the Hindoo population?

'With regard to the first point, I beg to state that the practice of removing sick people, particularly of advanced age, to the river-side, prevails generally in the Gangetic portion of Lower Bengal, and is considered by their nearest relatives as a duty incumbent upon them. I quote in a separate paper authorities from Shasters which have given rise to the practice, and show its necessity for spiritual advantage. From the purport of the texts quoted, His

Honour will observe that the custom of taking the sick to the river-side, that they may die with one-half of their body immersed in the water and the other half placed on the bank, is enjoined by religion.

'In reply to the second point, permit me to state that I never heard of an instance in which the practice was used as a means of getting rid of persons who were obnoxious or troublesome to their relatives, and I do not believe that such a means is adopted for the purpose, when numerous easier means, such as poisoning, or administering poisonous medicines, may be had recourse to to get rid of such persons. Nor have I ever heard that a descendant or relation has been prompted to participate in such an inhuman and unnatural deed for securing reversionary interest, not to say that it is contrary to religious injunctions and checked by worldly fear.

'With reference to the third point, I have to say that I know of several cases, some even in my own family, of the return home of the sick men from the river-side, when they were removed and immersed in the river water hastily, or by the advice of uneducated physicians, but they were never excluded from caste. The only ceremony observed on such occasions is the offering of poojah to the Ganges, or other presiding deity of the river.

'The Hindoos believe in the efficacy of a river-side death, but the destruction of human life is deemed so heinous an offence that the one has no connexion with the other. The object of river-side death is eternal happiness of the deceased, and not the commission of the atrocious crime of the destruction of human life.

'In answer to the fourth point, I beg to state that the practice in question is so much rooted in the minds of the Hindoos, whether intelligent or not, by usage, custom, and the injunction of the Shasters, that any authoritative interference would be distasteful to and considered by all of them as the exercise of a power by the ruling authorities. The word "intelligent" is very vague and bears an extensive meaning, but it cannot be concluded that men of intelligence will look without dissatisfaction upon the abolition of a time-honoured practice, especially as it is a duty incumbent on the relations for the spiritual welfare and faith of the dying, that is performed without violating the rules of natural law.

'In conclusion, I beg to observe that the mind of the community is not yet prepared for the abolition of the practice; but the time will come when education will exercise greater influence over the Hindoos, and when they themselves will gradually discourage such practices, first, by strictly adhering to the spirit of the tenets of the Shasters, and then restricting the observance to persons of advanced age. The observance will be spared in the case of sick young persons, who are now in a great many instances not precipitately removed to the river-side. From the time of the celebrated reformer Raja Ram Mohun Roy (I had the honour of being his coadjutor), I always entertained the opinion: —Let us begin the good work, and, as education spreads, the gradual disappearance of all objectionable superstitious practices will be the necessary result. Any authoritative interference will only make the people more obstinate in their adherence to the practice. Let the matter be left in the hands of the schoolmaster, who is already abroad and doing well, and the object will be eventually gained. His Excellency the Governor-General has very justly doubted whether much weight can be attached to the article in the *Dacca Prokash*. It may be known to you that there are two newspapers in the town of Dacca; one is called the *Hindoo Hitoishini*, and the other the *Dacca Herald*. The former is the organ of the orthodox Hindoos, and the latter that of the Brahmos. The majority of the inhabitants belong to the orthodox section of the community. Their opinion should not, therefore, be lightly treated and their feelings disrespected.'

A similar view is expressed by him in a letter to the Maharaja of Burdwan, on the subject of a Bill which that nobleman proposed to introduce for the suppression of Kulin polygamy,

After observing that the Bill would be unlikely to receive support, Prosunna Coomar writes · 'I do not think a body politic ought to be allowed to interfere with our domestic concerns, however objectionable they may be in principle. Education and change of the habits, notions, and ideas of the people will suppress polygamy, and it has been gradually suppressed to a large extent.'

In the month of June 1866, Prosunna Coomar Tagore was created a Companion of the Star of India, and he was present at the Viceregal Durbar at Agra in November of the same year.

This was his last visit to the North-Western Provinces. Early in the following year his health began again to fail, and a severe attack of rheumatism confined him to his house. In October, his continued indisposition compelled him to resign the membership of the Bengal Council. So anxious, however, was the Government to do him honour, that, in December. he was, notwithstanding, appointed a member of the Legislative Council of the Viceroy, the privilege of the private *entrée* to Government House having been conferred on him some days previously.

In the attainment of this honour he felt that his highest ambition was fulfilled, and the letters which he wrote to his friends on the occasion show that he still expected to be able to do some service to his country in his new capacity. So anxious was he to take part in the work of legislation that he abandoned a projected visit to Monghyr to enable him to attend the winter session. But his desire was not to be gratified. For early in the following year he grew so much worse that he was unable to take his seat, and was at last obliged to obtain leave of absence, first for a month, and then for the remainder of the session.

Every remedy that European or Native skill could devise, including even the milk of the camel, was called into service, but without material benefit to the patient.

On July 22 we find him, in what was destined to be his last letter to his old friend Mr. Dalrymple, writing : 'I am very weak. I don't think I shall be able to visit Monghyr.'

On August 18 his nephew writes to a friend that he is somewhat better. But the improvement was of short duration, and on the 30th of the same month he breathed his last.

The disposition which he made of his private estate by will was typical of the man and worthy of his great reputation. The legacies and bequests for religious, charitable, and educational purposes amounted to nearly seven lakhs of rupees.

The largest of these was a sum of three lakhs of rupees left in trust to the Calcutta University for the foundation of a law professorship, to be called the ' Tagore Law Professorship,' 10,000 rupees to be paid annually as salary to the Professor, and the residue to be applied to the printing of the lectures, and the gratuitous distribution of at least 500 copies of each course. To the District Charitable

Society he left 10,000 rupees; and a similar sum to the Calcutta Native Hospital.

For the maintenance of a hospice and dispensary, and for the service of the temple at Mulajore, he left a lakh of rupees, besides the estate of Mulajore and the surrounding villages, yielding an income of 16,000 rupees a year; and a sum of 35,000 rupees was further set apart for the erection of a building for the accommodation of the Sanskrit College at the same place, already mentioned. To various dependents he bequeathed upwards of a lakh of rupees.

But perhaps the noblest of all the provisions of the will was one by which the deceased left a sum of 100 rupees for every rupee of monthly salary to all his servants of ten years' standing or upwards, and a sum of fifty rupees for every rupee of monthly salary to all his servants of five years' standing and upwards.

His vast landed estates he bequeathed to the direct elder male representative of the senior branch for the time being of the family of his brother, Babu Hurro Coomar Tagore, and upon failure of his lineal male descendants, to the testator's own general heirs.

After a long and expensive litigation, the provisions of this will were, however, materially modified by the Privy Council.

On October 29, on the requisition of the British-Indian Association, a public meeting was held in the hall of that institution to do honour to the memory of Prosunna Coomar.

Among those present were Mr. John Cochrane, the Hon. Mr. Skinner, Mr. H. L. Dampier, Mr. J. B. Roberts, Mr. C. Paul, Mr. W. P. Davis, Mr. R. Turnbull, Mr. Orr, Raja Satto Charan Ghosal, Raja Norendra Krishna, Kumars Sattyananda Ghosal, Harendra Krishna, and Grish Chunder Singh; Babus Digumber Mitter, Doorga Churn Law, Peary Chand Mitter, Debendra Mullick, Rajendra Lal Mittra, Kishori Chand Mitter, Roma Nath Law, Koonja Lal Banerjea, Persad Dass Dutt, Persad Dass Mullick, Moulvi Abdul Luteef Khan Bahadur, Manockjee Rustomjee, Esq., Cowasjee Rustomjee, Esq., and many others.

On the motion of Raja Satto Charan Ghosal, the chair was taken by Mr. Cochrane, who read the following letters :—

' TO THE RAJA SUTYA SARAN GHOSAL BAHADOOR, C.S.I., Vice-President, B. I. A.

'Sobha Bazar Rajbaree, October 29, 1868.

' MY DEAR RAJA,—I have just received the printed letter, and much regret that uncertain health prevents my attendance at the public meeting, called by you this afternoon, to commemorate the good name of our citizen, the late lamented legislator, the Hon. Prosonno Coomar Thakoor, C. S. I., with whom I was intimately associated from the beginning.

' His public career as well as his private virtues are so well-known to the community, that it needs no support from me in the proceedings of the day. In conclusion, allow me to offer my mite of deep condolence to the Thakoor family for the personal bereavement.

' Trusting his memory is in the grateful

keeping of the meeting, under God's providence.

'I remain, yours faithfully,
'KALIKRISHNA, RAJA BR.'

'TO THE CHAIRMAN OF THE MEETING TO COMMEMORATE THE MEMORY OF HON. PROSONNA COOMAR TAGORE, C.S.I.

'Ooterparah, October 29, 1868.

'DEAR SIR.—I regret exceedingly that owing to ill-health I shall not be able to attend the meeting that has been called for to-day for the purpose of commemorating the memory of Hon. Prosonno Coomar Tagore, C.S.I., but I yield to no one in the grateful appreciation of the important public services which my late lamented friend rendered to our country, and in deploring the national loss which his death has created amongst us. From the commencement of his public career he was always a staunch and independent advocate of our political rights, and a zealous promoter in the cause of social reform. In the columns of his own paper (the *Reformer*) he first began to demand for the Natives those political rights some of which it was his delight in maturer years to see conferred on his countrymen, and also to impress on the people the necessity of a wide diffusion of education, which has since tended so much towards the progressive advancement of the nation. He took a principal part in the agitation which took place throughout this Presidency in consequence of the indiscriminate resumption of Lakhiraj lands by Government, and his exertions resulted in greatly modifying the severity of the Resumption Law. The benefit which he conferred on the country and on the Native Bar by enlisting himself as a member of the latter body, and raising the Bar to a position of dignity and independence, will be long remembered. He was one of the original projectors and afterwards one of the active members of the Landholders' Society and also of the British-Indian Association, and there was scarcely a movement during the last forty years, either for the assertion of the political rights or for the social advancement of the people, in which he was not either the originator or one of its warmest supporters. The assistance which he rendered to Government, both in his capacity as Clerk Assistant to the late Legislative Council and as a Member of the Bengal Council, and by his written opinions to different officers of Government, must have been invaluable from the intimate acquaintance he had with the condition of every class of the Native community, and the extensive store of information which he possessed on all subjects connected with the administration of the country, and which he used on all occasions with a power of generalisation and a clearness of judgment which are rare even in this age of intellectual advancement. His princely public donations and his private charities are also well known, and his contributions to the Hindoo legal literature, and the depth of his knowledge of Indian law and procedure, had gained for him not unjustly the sobriquet of Lord Lyndhurst of Bengal. The death of such a man we cannot sufficiently deplore, and I shall be glad to subscribe to any measure which the meeting might adopt for doing honour to his memory. His death has been a personal loss to me, who have had the honour of associating with him and benefiting by his counsel for upwards of thirty years.

'In conclusion, I beg to request the favour of your submitting this expression of my views to the meeting.

'Yours very truly,

'JOYKISSEN MOOKERJEA.'

The Chairman having addressed the meeting in a speech in which he bore testimony to the high character of the deceased; to his persistent advocacy of the rights, and his constant efforts to promote the education, of his countrymen; to his kindness and liberality, especially to his dependents, and to the benevolent injunctions he had left regarding the protection of the tenantry on his estates, Kumar Sattyanand Ghosal moved the first resolution :—

'That this meeting desires to record its deep sense of sorrow at the death of the late

Hon. Prosonno Coomar Tagore, C.S.I., who by his eminent abilities as a lawyer, thorough knowledge of the condition and wants of the Native community, large experience, active co-operation in all public matters, great social influence, and liberal support of projects of general usefulness, rendered services which entitle his memory to the grateful respect of the Indian public.'

The motion was seconded by Babu Rajendralala Mitra, in an eloquent and feeling speech, and, being put, was carried by acclamation.

The second resolution was moved by Raja Norendra Krishna :—

'That a marble bust of the late Hon. Prosonno Coomar Tagore, C.S.I., be placed in the hall of the British-Indian Association as a memorial of his eminent public services, and that public subscriptions be invited in furtherance of this subject.'

This resolution, which was seconded by Babu Kishori Chand Mitter, was also carried, and a Committee formed to carry it out;

and the bust referred to in it now adorns the Calcutta Town Hall.

Prosunna Coomar Tagore collected, at great cost, one of the finest legal libraries in the country, which is now in the possession of his nephew, the Hon. Maharaja Jotendra Mohun Tagore, Bahadur, C.S.I., and which contains many rare Oriental works not easily procurable elsewhere.

He left one son, Ganendra Mohun Tagore, who is a convert to Christianity, and was disinherited by his father.

Hurry Mohun Tagore.

Hurry Mohun Tagore, the fourth son of Darpa Narayan, was celebrated for his piety and his strict adherence to Hindoo religious usages. He daily offered oblations to fire, and performed certain arduous Brahminical ceremonies.

Bishop Heber, who on one occasion visited his country-house, thus describes his impressions in one of his letters :—

'I have become acquainted with some of

the wealthy Natives of whom I spoke, and we are just returned from passing the evening at one of their country-houses. This is more like an Italian villa than what one should have expected at the residence of Baboo Hurree Mohun Thakoor. Nor are his carriages, the furniture of his house, or the style of his conversation of a character less decidedly European. He is a fine old man, who speaks English well, is well informed on most topics of general discussion, and talks with the appearance of much familiarity on Franklin, chemistry, natural philosophy, &c. His family is Brahminical and of singular purity of descent; but about four hundred years ago, during the Mahommedan invasion of India, one of his ancestors having become polluted by the conquerors intruding into his zenanah, the race is conceived to have lost claim to the knotted cord, and the more rigid Brahmins will not eat with them. Being, however, one of the principal landholders in Bengal, and of a family so ancient, they still enjoy to a great degree the veneration of the common people, which the present head of the house appears to value, since I can hardly reconcile in any other manner his philosophical studies and imitation of many European habits, and the daily and austere devotion which he is said to practise towards the Ganges (in which he bathes three times every twenty-four hours), and his veneration for all the other duties of his ancestors. He is now said, however, to be aiming at the dignity of Raja, a title which at present bears pretty well the same estimation here as a peerage in England, and is conferred by Government in almost the same manner.

'The house is surrounded by an extensive garden, laid out in formal parterres of roses, intersected by straight walks, with some fine trees, and a chain of tanks, fountains, and summer-houses not ill-adapted to a climate where air, water, and sweet smells are almost the only natural objects which can be relished during the greater part of the year.

'There are also swings, whirligigs, and other amusements for the females of his family, but the strangest was a sort of "Montagne Russe" of masonry, very steep, and covered with plaster, down which the ladies used to *slide.* Of these females, however, we saw none—indeed, they were all staying at his town-house in Calcutta. He himself received us, at the head of a whole tribe of relations and descendants, on a handsome flight of steps, in a splendid shawl by way of mantle, with a large rosary of coral set in gold, leaning on an ebony crutch with a gold head. Of his grandsons, four very pretty boys, two were dressed like English children of the same age; but the round hat, jacket, and trousers by no means suited their dusky skins so well as the splendid brocade caftans and turbans covered with diamonds which the two elder wore. On the whole, both Emily and I have been greatly interested with the family, both now and during our previous interviews. We have several other Eastern acquaintances, but none of equal talent, though several learned Moollahs and one Persian doctor, of considerable reputed sanctity, have called on me.'

The account given by the Bishop of the circumstance owing to which the ancestors of the Tagores were held to have forfeited their title to wear the Brahminical thread differs somewhat, it will be seen, from that given in the earlier part of this Memoir, and there is a conflict of tradition on the subject which, at this distance of time, it would be impossible to decide with certainty.

The suspicion apparently entertained by him that the austerity of Hurry Mohun Tagore's worship of the Ganges was dictated by regard for Native opinion rather than by conviction, is opposed to all that is known of his character.

Hurry Mohun was an advocate of the practice of Suttee, and, on the occasion of a meeting of Hindoo gentlemen, held for the purpose of voting an address of thanks to Lord Hastings, on the eve of his departure from Bengal, he seconded an amendment, proposed by Babu (afterwards Raja) Radha Kanta Deb, that Lord Hastings should be specially thanked for the protection and encouragement he had given to that rite. The amendment was, however, rejected by a large majority.

In 1824 Bishop Heber gave a grand evening party at his house, at which Lord and Lady Amherst, and also a large number of Native gentlemen of rank were present. Hurry Mohun Tagore was among the guests, and was introduced by Bishop Heber to the Chief Justice. A discussion arose during the evening on the subject of the seclusion of Hindoo women, in which the Bishop, Hurry Mohun, and Radha Kanta Deb all took part; the Bishop arguing that the custom was not sanctioned by ancient Hindoo usage, but had been introduced after the Mahommedan invasion, and Hurry Mohun replying that it was too late now, after so many centuries, to think of going back to old customs, while Radha Kanta Deb insisted on the necessity of education as a condition precedent of the abandonment of the existing usage.

A curious story is told of the recovery of Hurry Mohun from a dangerous illness with which he was attacked during a visit to his estates in Dinajpur.

After he had been given up by all the attendant Kobirajes, and removed into the open air, according to Hindoo custom to die, an old woman suddenly appeared on the scene and offered to cure him if he were placed under her care. As there appeared to be no other hope, his attendants consented, whereupon the old woman punctured the top of the patient's head with a sharp fish-bone and applied a small quantity of some grey powder to the wound. Strange to say, in about an hour's time Hurry Mohun recovered his senses, and in a few days he was completely restored to health.

Out of gratitude he settled a large piece of land in perpetuity on the old woman whom he believed to have effected the marvellous cure.

Hurry Mohun left an only son, Wooma Nundun Tagore, more familiarly known as Nundo Lal Tagore, who was distinguished for his scholarship, and, like his father, was a staunch adherent of orthodox Hindooism. He attacked the theistic views of Ram Mohun

Roy in a work called the 'Pashundo Puran,' and was answered by the great reformer in the *Pathya Pradhan*.

He possessed also, in a conspicuous degree, the passion for music that seems to have been hereditary in the family, and was himself an accomplished singer and player on the *sitar*. The musicians of Calcutta looked upon him as their patron, and at the festival of *Basanta Pànchami* annually assembled in his house and presented him with the *Basanta gadwa*, an offering made by votaries of the art to their patrons, and consisting of a brass or earthenware vase, surmounted with fresh mangoe leaves and yellow flowers, emblematical of spring, and years of corn, symbolising plenty.

He is said, too, to have been the Bengali Beau Brummel of his time, and was recognised as the leader of fashion in matters of dress.

He left three sons, Lalit Mohun, Woopendra Mohun, and Brojendra Mohun.

The former was of a retiring disposition, and devoted his time largely to the study of the Hindoo violin, on which he attained to great proficiency. He again, left two sons, Judoo Nundun and Raghoo Nundun, the latter of whom is still living.

Woopendra Mohun, the second son of Wooma Nundun, who also is still living, mixed a great deal in English society in his younger days, but, owing to the state of his health, has long retired from active life.

Brojendra Mohun, the youngest son, was an excellent man of business, and managed the paternal estates even during his father's lifetime. He died young, leaving an only son, Anunda Mohun, who studied for the law and was enrolled as a pleader of the High Court, but, owing to ill-health, never practised. He was well known for his fondness for literature, and for the excellent library which he possessed and placed freely at the disposal of his numerous friends.

The youngest son of Darpa Narayan was Mohini Mohun Tagore, who died at an early age, but not without acquiring a great reputation for liberality. He bequeathed a sum of

Rs. 64,000 for the building of a temple, which is at present deposited in the High Court.

He left two sons, Kanay Lal and Gopal Lal, the latter of whom was well-known for his amiable character and his extensive charities, both private and public. At his death he bequeathed handsome sums of money to the District Charitable Society of Calcutta, the Mayo Hospital, the Fever Hospital, and the Police Hospital, and a lakh of rupees, together with land, for the building of a temple.

His son, Kally Kristo Tagore, who is still living, has followed in his father's footsteps, and is a large donor to most of the principal charities and educational institutions of the metropolis, including the District Charitable Society, the Mayo Hospital, the North Suburban Hospital, the Roman Catholic Orphanage, the Science Association (started by Dr. Mahendra Lal Sarkar), and the Oriental Seminary.

He is a man of liberal education and enlightened views, but, owing to bad health, he mixes but little in public life. He is, however, a skilful man of business, and one of the best and most popular landlords in the country.

JOTENDRA MOHUN TAGORE.

Huro Coomar Tagore, the eldest brother of Prosunna Coomar Tagore, had two sons, Jotendra Mohun Tagore, now the Hon. Maharaja Jotendra Mohun Tagore, Bahadur C.S.I., and the head of the family, and Sourendra Mohun Tagore, now Raja Sourendra Mohun Tagore, C.I.E.

Maharaja Jotendra Mohun Tagore was born in Calcutta in the year 1831. After acquiring the elements of a sound vernacular education at home, according to the custom of his family, he, when eight years of age, entered the Hindoo College, and continued his studies there till the age of seventeen. After leaving the College he completed his English education at home under the private tuition of Captain D. L. Richardson, the well-known scholar and poetical writer, the

Rev. Dr. Nash, and other competent European instructors.

Along with that devotion to Sanskrit studies which we have seen to have been hereditary in the family for a long series of generations, he displayed from an early period a marked taste for literary composition both in English and in the vernacular, and especially for poetry, as the verses contributed by him to the *Provakar*, then edited by the well-known Bengalee poet, Ishwar Chundra Gupta, and in the *Literary Gazette* testify.

At a comparatively early age he turned his special attention to the drama, and has not only, by his liberal patronage and personal exertion, done more than any man living to develop and raise the character of the Native stage, but has himself composed a large number of Bengalee dramas aud farces in the vernacular, among which the 'Bidya Sundara Natak' occupies the foremost place, and is entitled to rank among the classical compositions of the day.

His æsthetic taste soon led him to see that an improved orchestra was the necessary complement of an improved stage. Here his musical knowledge stood him in good stead, and, along with his brother, Sourendra Mohun Tagore, he applied himself with success to the task of developing a new system of concerted music, which has now been generally adopted for dramatic and other purposes.

He was largely instrumental in the organisation of the theatrical entertainments at the Belgatchia Villa which helped so much to popularise the Bengalee drama in its modern form, and thus paved the way for the establishment of public Native theatres.

Though theatrical performances by professional Native artistes are now, thanks to the stimulus thus given to the taste of the people, almost nightly occurrences in Calcutta, the private dramatic entertainments still given by the Maharaja in his house have not only lost none of their old attraction, but occupy a position of pre-eminence in the public estimation, and are attended by the *élite* of both the European and the Native community.

Maharaja Jotendra Mohun Tagore has been, from the commencement of his public career, an active member of the British Indian Association, and, after filling for some time the office of Honorary Secretary, he was, in 1879, elected its President.

In the beginning of the year 1870 Sir William Grey appointed him a Member of the Bengal Council, in which capacity he rendered such excellent service that in 1871 he was nominated for a further term of membership by Sir George Campbell.

The following letter, inviting him to retain office, testifies to the high opinion entertained of him by a Lieutenant-Governor who was above flattery :—

'Belvedere, Alipore, October 5, 1871.

' MY DEAR RAJA,—I hope you will allow me to nominate you for another term in the Bengal Legislative Council. Your high character and fair mode of dealing with all questions render your assistance especially valuable, and I have much confidence that you are a man not bound to class interests, but prepared to look to the good of the whole community, high and low alike.

'Believe me, very truly yours,

(Sd.) 'G. CAMPBELL.

'Raja Jotendra Mohun Tagore, &c.'

Previously to his retirement, Sir George Campbell's predecessor in office, Sir William Grey, had strongly recommended Jotendra Mohun to the Government of India for a suitable title, and on March 17, 1871, Lord Mayo accordingly conferred on him the rank of Raja Bahadur.

In making this recommendation, Sir William Grey wrote :—

'Babu Jotendra Mohun is a man of great enlightenment, and has had a thoroughly good English education. He is one of the leading members of the native community, is of unexceptionable private character, and is held by his fellow countrymen in the highest respect. He is a useful member of the Council of the Lieutenant-Governor, and takes a deep and thoughtful interest in the progress of the country. He has estates in the districts of Midnapore, Faridpore, Moorshadabad, Rajshahye, Nuddea, and the Twenty-four Pargannas, and during his lifetime enjoys the revenue of the large estates of the late **Rai Prosunna Coomar** Tagore in **Rungpore** and other places. He has always been found ready to contribute liberally to schools, roads, and other objects of public interest, both in Calcutta and in the districts in which his estates are situated, and has helped to promote science and literature amongst his countrymen by large contributions to that end. He regularly maintains eighteen poor students in Calcutta, and he fully accepted the obligation of his position in the famine, 1866, remitting the rents of his ryots, and feeding 250 paupers daily in Calcutta for a period of three months.'

The ceremony of investiture was performed by Sir George Campbell, who thus addressed Raja Jotendra Mohun Tagore on the occasion :—

'I have to convey to you the high honour which His Excellency the Viceroy, as the representative of Queen Victoria, has been pleased to confer on you. I feel a peculiar pleasure in being thus the channel of conveying this honour to you.

'You come from a family great in the annals of Calcutta, I may say great in the annals of the British dominions in India, conspicuous for loyalty to the British Government and for acts of public beneficence

'But it is not from consideration of your family alone the Viceroy has been pleased to confer the high honour upon you. You have proved yourself worthy of it by your own merits. Your great intelligence and ability, distinguished public spirit, high character and the services you have rendered to the State deserve a fitting recognition.

'I have had the pleasure of receiving your assistance as a member of the Bengal Council, and can assure you that I highly appreciate the ability and information which you bring to bear upon its deliberations. Indeed, nothing can be more acceptable to me than advice from one like yourself. It is true we have had occasion to differ, and honest differences of opinion will always prevail between man and man; but, at the same time, I can honestly tell you that when we have been on the same side, I have felt your support to be of the utmost value, and, when you have chanced to be in opposition, yours has been an intelligent, loyal, and courteous opposition.'

The liberal measures of relief mentioned in the above address as having been adopted by the Raja on his estates in Midnapore during the famine of 1866 gained for him the special thanks of the Government.

At the assemblage held at Delhi on January 1, 1877, on the occasion of the assumption of the Imperial title by Her Majesty the Queen, the title of Maharaja* was further conferred on him by Lord Lytton, the *sanad*

---

* This title was recognised as hereditary on January 1, 1891.

being presented to him by Sir Ashley Eden at a durbar at Belvedere, in which he occupied the place of honour, on August 14 following.

In the meantime, on February 1 of the same year, the Maharaja had been appointed a Member of the Legislative Council of the Governor-General; and so valuable was the assistance rendered by him in the deliberations of the Council, especially in the discussion of the provisions of the Civil Procedure Bill, that he was reappointed in 1879.

In the course of the debate on the above Bill, Sir A. Hobhouse, the Legal Member of Council, said:—

'Whatever can be said on that subject will be said by my friend Maharaja Jotendra Mohun Tagore; for in Committee he has supported the views of the objectors with great ability and acuteness, and I must add with equal good feeling and moderation.' And again: 'If the clause stood as in Bill No. IV., I confess I should not be able to maintain my ground against such an argument as we have heard from my honourable friend, Maharaja Jotendra Mohun Tagore. I have shown that conviction in the most practical way by succumbing to his arguments in Committee, and voting with him on his proposal to alter Bill No. IV.'

On July 28 in the same year, Maharaja Jotendra Mohun Tagore was created a Companion of the Order of the Star of India.*

He is also a Justice of the Peace for the Town of Calcutta, Fellow of the University of Calcutta, Trustee of the Indian Museum, and Governor of the Mayo Hospital.

Besides inheriting extensive landed property from his father, the Maharaja holds for life the usufruct of the estates of the late Prosunna Coomar Tagore, and is thus a large landholder in as many as a dozen different districts of Bengal. The population on his various estates is estimated to aggregate nearly 600,000 souls; and the revenue he

---

* The Maharaja was made a Knight Commander of the aforesaid Order on May 24, 1882. On January 1, 1890, the title of Maharaja Bahadur was conferred upon him.

pays to Government amounts to between three and four lakhs of rupees a year.

The Maharaja is a liberal donor and subscriber to most of the public institutions of Calcutta, and made a free gift to the Trustees of his interest in the land on which the new Chandny Hospital at Pathariaghatta is built.

Among the services which he has rendered to the cause of Native education is the foundation of two scholarships of Rs. 20 each, one for Sanskrit, in the name of his father, Huro Coomar Tagore, and the other for law, in the name of his uncle, Prosunna Coomar Tagore and a further scholarship for Sanskrit, of the value of Rs. 8 *per mensem*, in the name of Prosunna Coomar Tagore.

His country seat, the ' Emerald Bower,' where he had the honour of entertaining General Grant, the ex-President of the United States, during his late visit to Calcutta, is one of the most handsomely furnished villas in the neighbourhood of the metropolis, and contains a collection of paintings which is probably the finest in India.

Sourendra Mohun Tagore.

Huro Coomar Tagore's second son, Sourendra Mohun Tagore, now Raja Sourendra Mohun Tagore, C.I.E., whose learned investigations into the theory, and efforts for the advancement of the art, of Hindoo music have secured him a world-wide reputation and an unprecedented number of honorary distinctions from the governments and from learned societies of almost every civilised country, was born in the year 1840.

At the age of nine he entered the Hindoo College, where he remained nine years. While still a schoolboy, he displayed unusual literary talent, and at the age of fifteen wrote a concise outline of the history and geography of Europe, which was published in the year 1857, under the title of 'Bhugol o Itihas ghatita Brittanto,' while a year later he produced an original drama in the vernacular, entitled the 'Muktabali Natak,' and sometime afterwards a translation into Bengali of the 'Malabikagnimitra' of Kali Das.

At about the same age he commenced the study of the art to which the greater part of his subsequent leisure may be said to have been devoted, and, after mastering its elements, took lessons under the well-known teachers Latchmi Prasad Misr, and Professor Khettra Mohan Goswami.

Convinced that any advance on existing methods must be based on comparative investigation, he applied himself to the study of English music also, and engaged a German professor to teach him the pianoforte.

With a view to a thorough examination of the different theories of music, he further made an extensive collection of the principal works on the subject, ancient and modern, European and Oriental. The result was the composition of the 'Sangit-Sara,' a work on the theory of music, compiled from ancient authorities, and a long series of musical treatises and original compositions.

Among these may be noticed:—

Jatiya Sangita Bishayaka Prostava, or a Discourse on National Music, in Bengali.

Yantra-Khettra-Dipika, or a treatise on the *Sitara*, containing precepts and examples on the rudiments of Hindoo Music, intended as an introduction to the study of the above instrument. Illustrated with various exercises and ninety-four airs arranged according to the present system of Hindoo notation.

Mridanga Manjari, a treatise on the *Mredanga* (a percussion instrument).

Ækatana, or the Indian Concert, containing the elementary rules of the Hindoo musical notation with a description of the signs most frequently used in airs intended for the Ækatana.

Harmonium-Sutra, or a treatise on the Harmonium. (Translation.)

Hindoo Music, from various authors. Part I. (Compilation.)

Hindoo Music, reprinted from the *Hindoo Patriot*, September 7, 1874.

Yantra-Kosha, or a Treasury of the Musical Instruments of ancient and modern India and of various other countries, in Bengali.

Victoria-Gitika, or Sanskrit Verses, celebrating the deeds and virtues of Her Most Gracious Majesty, Queen Victoria, and her predecessors, composed and set to music by the Author (with a translation.)

Sangıt-Sara-Sangraha, or Theory of Sanskrit Music, compiled from the ancient authorities, with various criticisms and remarks by the Author.

English Verses, set to Hindoo Music, in honour of His Royal Highness the Prince of Wales.

Prince Panchasat, or Fifty Stanzas in Sanskrit, in honour of His Royal Highness the Prince of Wales, composed and set to music by the Author (with a translation).

Six Principal Ragas, with a brief view of Hindoo Music and with their emblematical representations.

Victoria Samrajyan, or Sanskrit Stanzas (with a translation) on the various dependencies of the British Crown, each composed and set to the appropriate national music, in commemoration of the assumption by Her Most Gracious Majesty, Queen Victoria, of the Imperial title.

Of these, the volume on the six principal Ragas, composed with a view of imparting an idea of Indian melodies to the Prince of Wales, and handsomely illustrated with lithographic pictures of the Ragas, is, perhaps, the most interesting to the general reader.

The following notice of this work from the *Pall Mall Gazette* gives a good idea of its contents :—

Hindoo Music.*—In a quarto volume, handsomely illustrated with lithographic engravings by a Native artist, Doctor Sourindro Mohun Tagore has taken in hand to give a lucid

---

* *Six Principal Rayas, with a Brief View of Hindoo Music.* By Sourindro Mohun Tagore, Mus. Doc., Calcutta, 1875.

exposition of the origin and characteristics of Hindoo music. To begin with the beginning, the Sanskrit word *sángita* has the three-fold signification of song, percussion, and dancing. The works that describe the principles and laws of vocal and instrumental music and of all kinds of spectacular entertainments are called *sángita sastras*. From the scientific point of view, a *sángita sastra* may be considered as treating 'of the origin and propagation of *nada*, or sound; of the doctrine of *srutis*, or the theory of Sanskrita intervals; of the doctrine of *swaras*, or musical sounds; of the formation of the different species of scales; of the rules of *murchchhanas* and *tanas*; of the composition of *ragas* and their various modifications and variations; of the variety of *talas*, or times conformable to regular metre; and of the rules and directions with respect to the various styles of theatric representation, considered as an art. It lays down the necessary directions for the cultivation of the human voice, for the performance of instrumental music, and for the various motions and gestures in dancing' There are two kinds of *sángita*, the one of divine origin, and therefore universally venerated; the other secular, and reflecting the peculiar habits, customs, and feelings of the tribe or people out of whose daily life it has sprung into existence. In these degenerate days, however, little regard is paid to the severe rules touching *ragas* and *raginis* laid down by Sanskrit authorities; while dancing has long since ceased to be a moving presentment of 'sacred love and affection' such as animated the heart of the ancient Hindoos.'

. . . .

The mystery of Hindoo music consists largely in its *srutis*, or minute intervals, distinctly perceptible to an Indian ear, but which the duller European organism fails to appreciate. There are twenty-two kinds of *sruti* to each *saptaka*, or octave, the compass of the Hindoo scale being limited to three octaves of seven notes each. Strictly speakng, it is understood that no human voice can compass more than two-and-a-half *saptakas*, and that consequently has become the limit of instrumental music. A *sruti* is a quarter-tone, or the third of a tone, according to its position in the scale. In the arrangements of intervals it is admitted that Sanskrit writers were not mathematically accurate, but on the other hand, it is contended that 'sense and a 'well-cultivated ear' are more necessary than mathematies for the comprehension of music. The aggregate result of a number of *srutis* is called a *swara* or musical sound, and is said to exercise 'a calm and soothing influence on the ear.' In number the Hindoo notes are the same as those of western nations, and their initial letters serve to exhibit the gamut or *saptaka*, which, though called an octave, has actually only seven notes, *sa, ri, ga, ma, pa, dha, ni*. These various gradations of sound are supposed to have been derived from the cries of animals and the songs of birds. The first, *sa*, say the Sanskrit writers, 'was imitated from the call of the peacock;' the second, *ri*, 'from the bellowing of the ox;' the third *ga*, 'from the bleeting of the goat;' the fourth *ma*, 'from the howling of the jackal, or from the voice of the crane,' the fifth, *pa*, 'from the call of the blackbird, called *kokhilla*;' the sixth, *dha*, 'from the sound of the frog, or from the neighing of the horse;' and the seventh, *ni*, 'from the noise of the elephant.' The imitations are happily more melodious than the originals. Flats and sharps are respectively named *komala* and *tivra*, and are produced by raising or depressing a note the value of one or two *srutis*. The difference between the *vikrita swaragrama* of the Hindoos (the seven notes of the *saptaka* form twelve *vikritas*; and the English chromatic scale lies in this—that the former proceeds by semitones and *srutis*, and the latter by a regular succession of semitones. The early Sanskrit writers ranged the notes under four castes— Brahmans, Kshatriyas, Vaisyas, and Sudras—corresponding to the major tones, minor tones, semitones, and the chromatic notes of western music. The predominant character of Hindoo music being melody, harmony is regarded as altogether insignificant, though occasionally used for quite exceptional purposes. Passing over an extremely learned disquisition on the nature and attributes of *murchchhanas*, seven of which belong to each *saptaka*, or octave of seven notes, we come to the *tala* or Hindoo time. A *tala*, which literally means the beating of time by the clapping of hands, is 'metrically divided by a certain arrangement of *matras*,' and it takes four *matras* to constitute a measure

Several pages having been devoted to showing what a *raga* is not, the reader is at length informed that it 'signifies an effect on the mind produced by the agreeable relation of successive notes, each *raga* having some affinity with a certain feeling or affection of the mind.' The sentiments they are supposed to illustrate are love, mirth, tenderness, anger, heroism, terror, disgust, and surprise. They are usually sung once in their simple form, and then repeated with variations. In the formation of a *raga* at least five notes are required, and when rhythm is imparted it receives the character of *gita*, a name applied to 'all measured strains of music, whether vocal or instrumental.' The six original *ragas*, whose names need hardly be transcribed, 'are restricted for their performance to particular times and seasons. They are each represented as a demigod, wedded to six *raginis* or nymphs.'

. . . .

To attempt to give an intelligible idea of the Indian system of notation would require far more space than the subject deserves; but it may be stated that only one line is used, with the initials of the seven notes and with certain subsidiary signs.

From a scientific point of view, the highest value probably attaches to the 'Sangit-Sara-Sangraba,' which teems with quotations from the Sanskrit classics, and the 'Yantra-Kosha,' which contains a full account, in

Bengali, of the construction of the musical instruments of various countries in ancient and modern times, both of which works have been very highly praised by the learned Professor Weber.

Much as Raja Sourendra Mohun Tagore has done to promote a knowledge of Hindoo music by the publication of these works, his greatest service to the cause has been his establishment of the Bengal Music School, an institution for the teaching of Hindoo music on scientific principles, which is fast placing the practice of the art in Bengal on a sound footing, and has already popularised its study to an extent hitherto unknown in India in modern times.

This institution, which has been founded and maintained entirely at the expense of the Raja, was opened on August 3, 1781. To it is attached a branch school, called the Kolhutolah Branch Musical School, and also maintained at the expense of the Raja.

The students, who are taught by competent professors, are charged only a nominal fee, and valuable prizes are awarded at the periodical examinations.

The Raja himself frequently visits the school and displays the greatest interest in its progress. The annual musical festival and distribution of prizes is attended by large numbers of Europeans interested in Native education, and its usefulness has been recognised in the warmest manner by the educational authorities of the country, and by successive Viceroys and Lieutenant - Governors, as well as by Her Majesty the Queen-Empress herself, in a certificate presented to the Raja in her name by Sir Richard Temple.

Raja Sourendra Mohun Tagore's patronage of music and musical studies is not confined to his own school. He contributes a liberal monthly stipend for the maintenance of a teacher of music at the Calcutta Normal School, besides awarding annually two silver medals to the most successful students; supplies music-masters and musical books to numerous public and private schools at his own expense, and is always ready with his purse to encourage musical artistes and authors.

His efforts for the diffusion of a better knowledge of the principles and practice of Hindoo music abroad are no less conspicuous than his exertions for the promotion of the art at home. A mere enumeration of the governments, museums, learned societies, and universities that are beholden to him for collections of books on the subject, or of specimens of Indian musical instruments, would occupy several pages of this Memoir.

The following list of some of the orders, titles, distinctions and decorations conferred on him will convey an idea of the extent of his reputation :—

India.—Companion of the Order of the Indian Empire; *Sanad* of the Title of Raja, with *Khilat;* Certificate of Honour from the Government, as Founder of the Bengal Musical School; Fellow of the University of Calcutta; the gold Decoration of the Gurkha Star of Nepaul; Degrees of *Sangita Silpa-Bidyasagara* and *Bharatiya-Sangita-Nayaka* from Nepaul.

America.—Degree of Doctor of Music (April 1875).

England.—Member of the Royal Asiatic Society, and

Fellow of the Royal Society of Literature; Honorary Patron of the Society of Science, Letters, and Art, of London.

France.—Officer of the Academy, Paris; Officier de l'Instruction Publique, France; Honorary Member of the First Class of the Académie Montreal.

Portugal.—Chevalier of the Royal Potuguese Military Order of Christ.

Sardinia.—Patron of the Athenæum of the Royal University of Sassari.

Sicily.—Honorary Member of the Royal Academy, Palermo.

Italy.—Honorary Member of the Royal Academy of St. Cecilia, Rome; Honorary Member of the Societa Didascalica Italiana; Academic Correspondent of the Royal Musical Institute, Florence; Co-operating Member of the Academia Pittagorica, Naples (with a silver medal); Corresponding Member of the Royal Academy of Raffaelle, Urbino (with a medal); Honorary Member of the Philharmonic Academy of Bologna; Benemerito of the Royal University of Parma; Ordinary Member of the Oriental Academy, Florence; Corresponding Member of the Royal Academy, Turin; Honorary Member of the Societa Operaria di Lucca; Gold medal from the Reale Societa Didascalica Italiana, Roma.

Switzerland.—Corresponding Member of the Geneva Institute.

Austria.—Commander of the Most Exalted Order of

Francis Joseph; Corresponding Member of the Oriental Museum, Vienna.

Saxony.—Knight Commander of the first class of the Order of Albert.

Belgium.—Knight Commander of the Order of Leopold; Associate Member of the Royal Academy of Science, Letters, and Fine Arts, Brussels.

Holland.—Foreign Member of the Royal Philological and Ethnographical Institution of Netherlands India at the Hague; Corresponding Member of the Society of Amsterdam.

Sweden.—Honorary Member of the Royal Musical Academy, Stockholm, with a gold medal.

Greece.—Honorary Member of the Archæological Society of Athens.

Turkey.—The Imperial Order of Medjidie of the second class from His Majesty the Sultan of Turkey.

Egypt.—Chevalier of the Imperial Order of Medjidie.

Ceylon.—Honorary Member of the Royal Asiatic Society, Ceylon.

Siam.—Decoration of the Order of Basabamala from His Majesty the King.

Java.—Corresponding Member of the Society of Arts and Sciences, Batavia, and a Medal struck on the occasion of the first centennial of the Society.

Australia.—Honorary Member of the Philharmonic Society of Melbourne.

Franc Chevalier of the Order of the Knights of the Holy Saviour, Montreal, Jerusalem, Rhodes, and Malta.

Knight of Honour of the Order Caballeros Hospitalaros of Spain.

First Class of the Celestial Imperial Order of the Precious Star of China.

High Protector of the Order of the Humanitarian Academy of the White Cross, Leghorn.

Cavalier of Honour of the Academic Order of Buenos Ayres (South America)

Honorary President of the Propaganda di Scienza Popolare, Naples; with a Gold Medal.

Imperial High Order of the Lion and Sun from His Imperial Majesty the Shah of Persia.

Fellow of Trinity College, London.

The Title of Nawab from His Imperial Majesty the Shahen Shah of Persia.

The list might be considerably extended and a still longer one made of the medals, acknowledgments, and complimentary presents of photographs, autographs, books and musical instruments, which the Raja has received from royal and eminent personages, and learned societies, in various parts of the world.

On January 1, 1880, Sourendra Mohun Tagore was invested with the Companionship of the Order of the Indian Empire, and on the third of the following month the title of Raja, long previously conceded him by courtesy, was formally conferred on him by Lord Lytton, whose warm personal congratulations he received on both these occasions.

Besides the works already mentioned, Raja Sourendra Mohun Tagore is the author of the 'Eight Principal Rasas of the Hindoos' a translation of the *Veni Sanhara Natak*, or 'Binding of the Braid;' *Rome Kavya*, a poetical history of Rome, from its foundation to the present day, in Sanskrit; and the *Manimala*, a voluminous and learned polyglot work on gems, compiled from various sources, Oriental and European, and replete with curious as well as practical information.

Raja Sourendra Mohun Tagore is an Honorary Magistrate and Justice of the Peace for the Town of Calcutta, and is joint owner, with his brother, of the vast hereditary estates which have already been mentioned in the Memoir of the latter.

He has two sons, Kumar Promodh Tagore

and Kumar Pradyota Kumar Tagore,* the former of whom was married with great *éclat* on January 31, 1880, on which occasion the Raja presented the munificent sum of Rs. 8,000, besides large quantities of clothes, to the District Charitable Society of Calcutta.

---

* Pradyota Kumar has been adopted by Maharaja Bahadoor Sir Jotendro Mohun Tagore, K C S I.